COASTS

DEBBIE MILTON AND GERD MASSELINK
SERIES EDITORS: BOB DIGBY AND SUE WARN

© The Geographical Association, 2018

This book is copyright under the Berne Convention. All rights are reserved. Apart from any fair dealing for the purpose of private study, research, criticism or review, as permitted under the Copyright, Designs and Patents Act 1988, no part of this publication may be reproduced, stored in a retrieval system, or transmitted in any form or by any means, electronic, electrical, chemical, mechanical, optical, photocopying, recording or otherwise, without the prior written permission of the copyright owner. Enquiries should be addressed to the Geographical Association. The authors have licensed the Geographical Association to allow members to reproduce material for their own internal school/departmental use, provided that the authors hold the copyright. The views expressed in this publication are those of the authors and do not necessarily represent those of the Geographical Association.

ISBN 978-1-84377-412-9
First published 2018
Impression number 10 9 8 7 6 5 4 3 2 1
Year 2020 2019 2018

Published by the Geographical Association, 160 Solly Street, Sheffield S1 4BF
Company number 07139068
Website: www.geography.org.uk
E-mail: info@geography.org.uk
The Geographical Association is a registered charity: no 1135148

The Geographical Association (GA) is the leading subject association for all teachers of geography. Our charitable mission is to further geographical knowledge and understanding through education. Our journals, publications, professional events, website and local and online networks support teachers and share their ideas and practice. The GA represents the views of geography teachers and plays a leading role in public debate relating to geography and education.

The GA would be happy to hear from other potential authors who have ideas for geography books. You may contact the Head of Publications via the GA at the address above.

Cover image: Chapel Rock near Perranporth, Cornwall. Photo: © Darren Flinders, reproduced under Creative Commons licence CC BY-ND 2.0.
Copy edited by Diane Rolfe
Cartography/illustrations by Kim Farrington
Designed and typeset by Ledgard Jepson Ltd
Printed and bound in the UK by W&G Baird

Disclaimer: Every effort has been made to identify and contact the original sources of copyright material. If there have been any inadvertent breaches of copyright we apologise.

Contents

Editors' preface	4
Chapter 1 Coastal systems	5
Chapter 2 Coastal processes	10
Chapter 3 Rocky coasts	19
Chapter 4 Depositional coasts	24
Chapter 5 Sea-level change and coastal response	34
Chapter 6 Coastal management	42
Key terms	51

Editors' preface

The *Top Spec Geography* series is designed to be used by 16–19 year olds in schools and colleges. The writing teams, combining the expertise of a specialist in their field with that of an experienced classroom teacher, have been chosen to ensure that contemporary and exciting geography, which brings together the latest research and thinking on topical themes, is accessible to post-16 students.

Each book in the series consists of:
- written chapters, with illustrations and data that complement the text
- activities for use in groups and as guides for private study. Some activities are designed to encourage discussion, while others help to promote students' understanding of the issues
- background theory, to enable students to see the wider picture
- key information boxes
- ideas for further research: most post-16 teaching encourages students to become independent learners and some specifications have research units designed to help prepare students for this
- a glossary of key words and terms.

In addition, there are online resources which have been written to extend and complement the book, and will ensure that the most up-to-date research and data are available. Each chapter will remind you about these resources, which can be found at www.geography.org.uk/topspec.

Although the books have been written mainly with geography students in mind, the series may also prove useful for students:
- taking public examination or diploma courses in other subjects
- who want to read beyond their exam courses in order to apply or prepare for university
- looking at new topics in their first year of university.

Coasts

This book meets the requirements for the popular 'Coasts' option within the 'Landform systems' compulsory core of all four A level specifications in England and Wales, and will also be of use for those studying IB pre-U and international A level. The book includes:
- an analysis of how coastal systems operate and consideration of key concepts such as feedback, equilibrium and threshold
- an assessment of the role and relative importance of waves, tides and currents as part of the coastal processes that shape the coast both spatially and over time
- accurate and detailed explanation of how coastal processes form the coastal landforms found in both rocky (largely erosional) coasts and sandy depositional coasts, both with appropriate exemplification
- exploration of the complex issues relating to the role of sea-level changes and coastal response to them
- up-to-date information and the latest thinking on coastal management strategies.

The book is supported by suggestions for whole-class activities and ideas for individual further research using a range of websites, and provides detailed online case studies from the UK and further afield (including Lithuania, the Netherlands and Vietnam).

The author team combines the expertise of frontline university research with many years of lecturing at the UK's largest A level centre to give readers the confidence not only to handle exam questions but also to inspire them in their NEA research and fieldwork.

Bob Digby and Sue Warn
May 2017

Online resources

Each book in the *Top Spec Geography* series has a range of supplementary materials and resources including:
- extra information
- extended question lists
- model answers and mark schemes
- links to relevant websites
- extended glossaries
- photo galleries.

To access these go to **www.geography.org.uk/topspec** then click on the button for this book. You will then be asked for your password.

The unique password for this book is MM12E1

1. Coastal systems

Coastal environments are arguably the most important and intensely used of all areas settled by humans. The attractions of coastal locations have led approximately 44% of the global population to live within 150km of the coast and at less than 100m above sea level. As a result of rapid urbanisation, population density in coastal areas is three times larger than average, and projected population growth rates in the coastal zone are the highest in the world. Twenty-seven of the world's 35 megacities (i.e. those inhabited by more than 10 million people) can be considered coastal cities. Perhaps most disconcertingly, it is predicted that by 2060, 60% of the global population could occupy coastal floodplains that are at risk of a 1 in 100-year coastal flood event.

However, it is important to define what is meant by the term 'coast', because it can mean different things to different people. For most holidaymakers the coast is synonymous with the beach and the shallow sea; for birdwatchers the coast generally refers to the intertidal zone where birds tend to congregate; for some it is home, while for cartographers the coast is simply a line on a map defining the land at high tide. Look at Figure 1.1, which shows a gravel barrier with a freshwater lagoon behind. Can the lagoon be considered part of the coast?

The most commonly used term in coastal management is 'coastal zone'; but, even here, definitions differ widely (Information Box 1.1). If we accept Carter's definition (see Information Box 1.1) and consider it in the context of recent geological timescales and sea-level change, the landward limit of the coastal system would include the coastal depositional landforms and the marine erosion surfaces formed when the sea level was high (slightly above present-day sea level) during warm interglacial periods. During cold glacial periods, sea level was about 120m lower than present and thus coastal processes were close to the edge of the continental shelf.

Figure 1.1 Aerial view of the gravel barrier at Slapton Sands, South Devon, backed by a freshwater lagoon. **Photo:** © P. Ganderton.

> **INFORMATION BOX 1.1**
> **DEFINITIONS OF THE COASTAL ZONE**
>
> **The coastal zone is:**
> - 'The area between the landward limit of marine influence and the seaward limit of terrestrial influence.' (Carter, 1988)
> - 'the geomorphologic area either side of the seashore in which the interaction between the marine and land parts occurs in the form of complex ecological and resource systems made up of biotic and abiotic components coexisting and interacting with human communities and relevant socio-economic activities.' (Mediterranean ICZM Protocol, 2008)
> - 'Its precise delimitation depends directly on the problem posed initially. The limits should therefore extend into the sea and land just as far as required by the objectives of the management plan.' (UNESCO/IOC, 1997)
> - 'It could include areas affected by off-shore and near-shore natural processes, such as areas of potential tidal flooding and erosion; enclosed tidal waters, such as estuaries and surrounding areas of land; and areas which are directly visible from the coast. The inland limit of the zone will depend on the extent of direct maritime influences and coast-related activities. In some places, the coastal zone may be relatively narrow, such as where there are cliffs. Elsewhere, particularly where there are substantial areas of low-lying land and inter-tidal areas, it will be much wider.' (Defra, UK)

The seaward limit of the coastal system is, therefore, defined by the edge of the continental shelf, which typically occurs in water depths of 150m. With projected future sea-level rise, areas not currently coastal will become coastal, thus any definition should recognise the dynamic nature of the coast.

In the same way that definitions of the coast vary, a huge variety of terms are used to describe coastal features and processes. Figure 1.2 shows how the coast can be referred to in different ways, using either the shoreline position (backshore, foreshore, inshore and offshore) or a spatial differentiation related to the dominant wave processes (swash zone, surf zone and breaker zone), as seen on Fanore Beach in western Ireland (Figure 1.3).

The coastal system

The coast is a very dynamic environment and, arguably, one of the most geomorphologically active landscapes on Earth. It undergoes constant change that presents many challenges to residential, industrial, commercial and tourist developments. Possibly the most serious threat is that posed by sea-level rise (see Chapter 5). Studying the coast is very interdisciplinary and is also suited to a systems approach.

Fundamentally, a coastal system is made up of morphological components linked by flows of energy and materials. There are strong mutual links between processes and landforms. For example, an increase in energy during a storm may cause beach and dune erosion (processes are responsible for morphological change), but the eroded material may form subtidal bars that will focus the wave breaking and inhibit further beach and dune erosion (morphological change modifies the processes). Thus, there is feedback between the processes and morphology, and a system that exhibits such feedback is referred to as a 'process-response system'. The term 'morphodynamic system' is also used, where 'morpho' refers to morphology (shape) and 'dynamic' relates to hydrodynamic processes (waves and currents). Figure 1.4 shows three elements of a coastal morphodynamic system and the accompanying boundary conditions. These are:

1. Processes – hydrodynamic (tides, currents and waves) and aerodynamic processes (wind) supply changing amounts of energy to the system. All types of weathering processes – physical, chemical and biological – also contribute to sediment transport by either breaking down rock into fragments or weakening rock so that it is then broken down more easily by waves and currents.
2. Sediment transport – when sufficient energy allows the entrainment (carrying) of sediment in the water, material can then be transported along the coast. The resulting pattern of erosion and deposition can be assessed using the sediment budget (see Information Box 2.2, page 16). If more sediment enters a coastal region than leaves it, then the sediment balance is positive and deposition will occur, and the coastline may advance. A negative sediment balance occurs when more sediment leaves a coastal region than enters it and net erosion will follow, with possible coastline retreat.

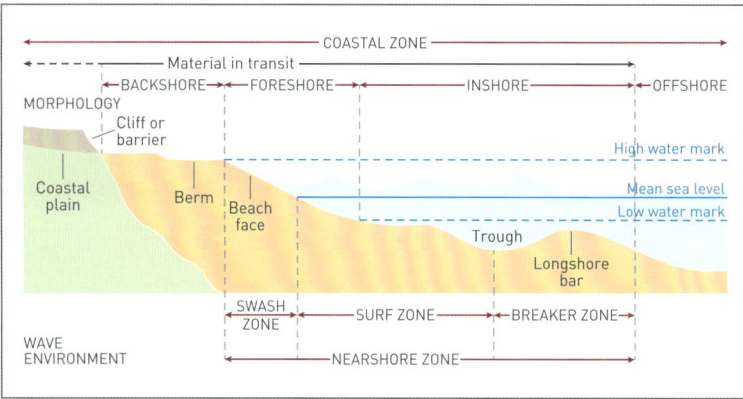

Figure 1.2 Subdivisions of the coastal zone. **Source:** Briggs et al., 1997.

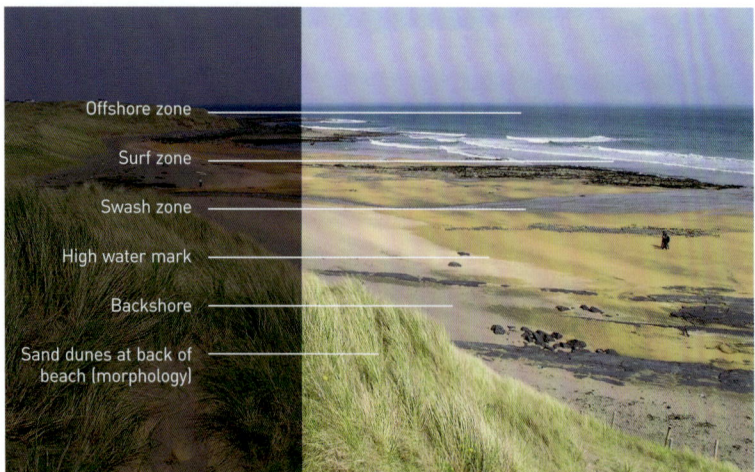

Figure 1.3 The coastal zone on Fanore beach on the west coast of Ireland, showing a wide intertidal zone with rock outcrops, and backed by extensive dune systems. **Photo:** © G. Masselink.

3. Morphology – the surface of a landform or assemblage of landforms such as coastal dunes, deltas, estuaries, beaches and shore platforms is referred to as the morphology. Changes in morphology are brought about by erosion and deposition. There is such a close interaction between morphology and processes that it is often unclear as to which determines which (the classic 'chicken-and-egg' problem). This makes it very difficult to predict coastal development over long timescales.

While these three elements (processes, sediment transport and morphology) are interconnected and work together within the coastal system, they are ultimately driven and controlled by environmental factors known as boundary conditions. The nature of the underlying geology will control the type and amount of sediment supply into the system. The dynamic conditions of wind, waves, storms and tides will affect the processes, and sea level determines where these processes operate within the system. Added to this could be human activity, because the building of coastal defences and beach nourishment has drastically changed coastal dynamics. In addition, human activities are causing climate change, which is responsible for at least part of the observed sea-level rise.

Equilibrium

Changing morphology due to fluctuating energy conditions occurs because the coastal system strives to achieve a balance with the processes operating within it, i.e. to be in equilibrium. There are three types of equilibrium (Figure 1.5):

- Steady state equilibrium: when energy levels do not vary far from the long-term average, then features such as beaches do not drastically change their gradients over time and appear to be constant. The system will display small fluctuations around the mean equilibrium condition.
- Meta-stable equilibrium: if a coast is hit by a major energy event (an extreme storm or tsunami), it can trigger a large change or shift to the system (for example, the development of a new tidal inlet cut through an existing barrier system as a result of a hurricane). It may appear that a new equilibrium is reached, but another major shift can occur, pushing the system back to where it was previously (for example, the closure of the newly-developed tidal inlet following a period of strong littoral drift). Thus, a meta-stable coastal system may switch between different equilibrium states at distinctly different levels.
- Dynamic equilibrium: when change is more gradual over time, such as sea-level rise or the addition of fluvial sediment to a deltaic system, the equilibrium position changes, but in a more measured manner. The system is trying to find its new position over time and may, in fact, never reach it.

It follows that because all the components within a system are interconnected, there will be feedback mechanisms that operate to bring the system to its new state or to maintain the system in its present state. The feedback between morphology and processes is fundamental to coastal morphodynamics, and can be *negative* or *positive*.

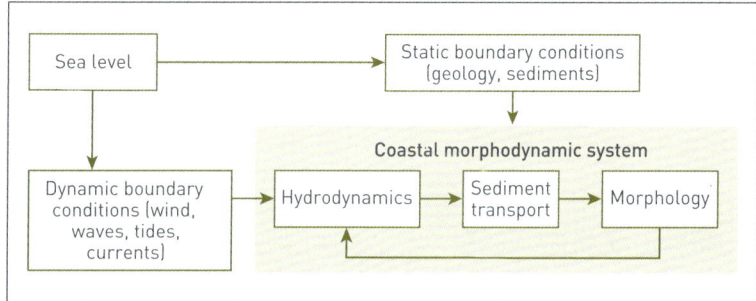

Figure 1.4 Coastal morphodynamic system with its static and dynamic boundary conditions. **Source:** Holden, 2008.

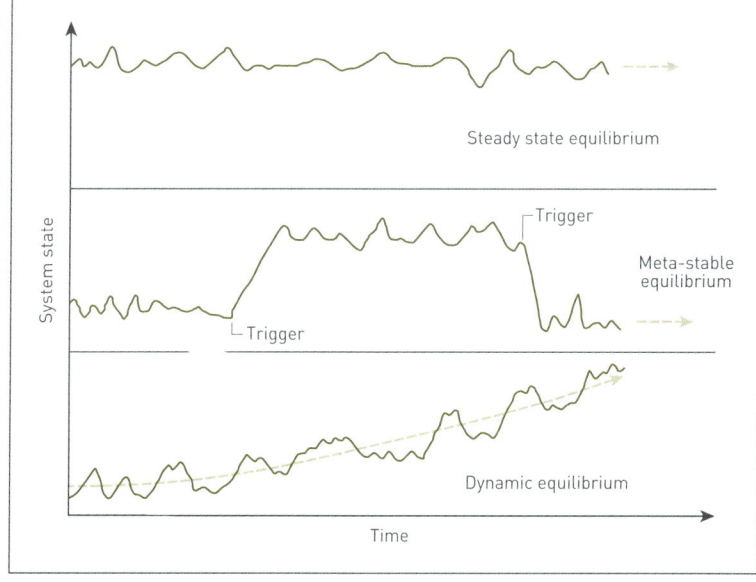

Figure 1.5 Different types of equilibrium: steady state, meta-stable and dynamic. **Source:** Briggs *et al.*, 1997.

- *A negative feedback* dampens the amount of coastal change and works to maintain a steady state. For example, salt marshes build up vertically due to sediment deposition during high tide. As the salt marsh develops, it will receive increasingly less sediment because the flooding frequency decreases. This will reduce the accretion rate until the salt marsh elevation has been optimised and no more deposition can occur.
- *A positive feedback* pushes a coastal system away from equilibrium and amplifies the initial change in the system. For example, if a storm breaks through a sand dune ridge, the dune will be susceptible to further lateral wind erosion, thus leading to fragmentation and a greater vulnerability to wave erosion in the next storm. The gap in the dune will not be 'fixed' until, for example, vegetation re-establishes itself and traps sediment.

Adjustment of coastal morphology to changing conditions involves a redistribution of sediment that requires time. The time required for the adjustment to occur is known as the relaxation time. The relaxation time strongly depends on the volume of sediment involved in the adjustment of morphology and is related to the size of the landform itself. Large coastal landforms (such as barriers or basins) have longer relaxation times than small morphological features (such as beach cusps or wave ripples). Generally, the relaxation time exceeds the time between changes in environmental conditions. It is, therefore, unlikely that a steady-state equilibrium is ever reached, particularly for large coastal landforms, and morphology is always playing catch-up.

A good example of the consequences of long relaxation times is the erosion of the east coast of England – in Norfolk and at Holderness in the East Riding of Yorkshire. These areas experience erosion rates of up to several metres per year, some of the largest in the UK. The current sea-level rise and its impact on the area's soft geology is often used to explain such high rates. However, these erosion rates have been occurring for thousands of years – in fact, since the sea level more or less reached its present-day position after the last ice age. The reality is that the coastline and the underwater profile of Holderness and Norfolk is markedly out of equilibrium with the current wave conditions and has been trying to find its new position for a very long time and will continue to do so for many more years.

Large-scale sediment cells

Coastal systems can be studied at any spatial scale, from microfeatures (such as beach cusps) to sections of coast many tens of kilometres long. In terms of time, one might study the movement of sediment ranging from seconds to decades. On a national scale, major sediment pathways around the coast of England and Wales have been recognised, and 11 major sediment 'cells' defined (Figure 1.6). The Department of Environment, Farming and Rural Affairs (Defra, 1993) defines a sediment cell as:

> 'A length of coastline and its associated nearshore area within which the movement of coarse sediment (sand and shingle) is largely self-contained. Interruptions to the movement of sand and shingle within one cell should not affect beaches in a neighbouring sediment cell.'

This suggests that each cell is a closed system, with headlands and peninsulas acting as barriers to sediment movement, and major estuaries as sinks. However, in reality, it is likely that there is some transfer of sediment between the cells, especially finer material carried in suspension, due to variations in winds and tidal currents.

These 11 main coastal sediment cells and their many sub-cells are key components of shoreline management plans (SMPs, see Chapter 6). Identification of these cells is useful because, if they are assumed to be closed systems, they can be managed as individual units. The production, transfer and storage (deposition) of sediment along the coast are key to coastal management – indeed, it has been said that coastal management is all about sediment management.

Figure 1.7 indicates the different sources and losses of sediment at a smaller scale. Sediment may be stored for a period of time, for example in sub-tidal bar systems, and is then reworked within the cell system. When prolonged calm conditions dominate, sub-tidal sediment is returned to the beach and dune systems. Alternatively, sediment can be taken out of circulation, for example, when it gets incorporated into vegetated dune systems or by human actions (such as dredging, or hard coastal management – see 'Sources of sediment', page 16). If the volume of sediment decreases, erosion will increase; conversely, deposition occurs if available sediment increases. Around the UK coast, sediment levels have been decreasing in the past few decades, resulting in narrower and steeper beaches. Possible reasons for these changes could be sea-level rise, lack of offshore material reducing replenishment, or artificial structures interrupting natural sediment pathways. The amount of sediment available in any sized cell can be calculated by its sediment budget (see Information Box 2.2, page 16).

As the coastal system evolves over time, its evolution is recorded in the sediments (clay, silt, sand and gravel) in the form of the stratigraphy. It is important to realise that stratigraphic sequences are a record of the depositional history and that erosional events are represented only by gaps in the stratigraphic record.

COASTS

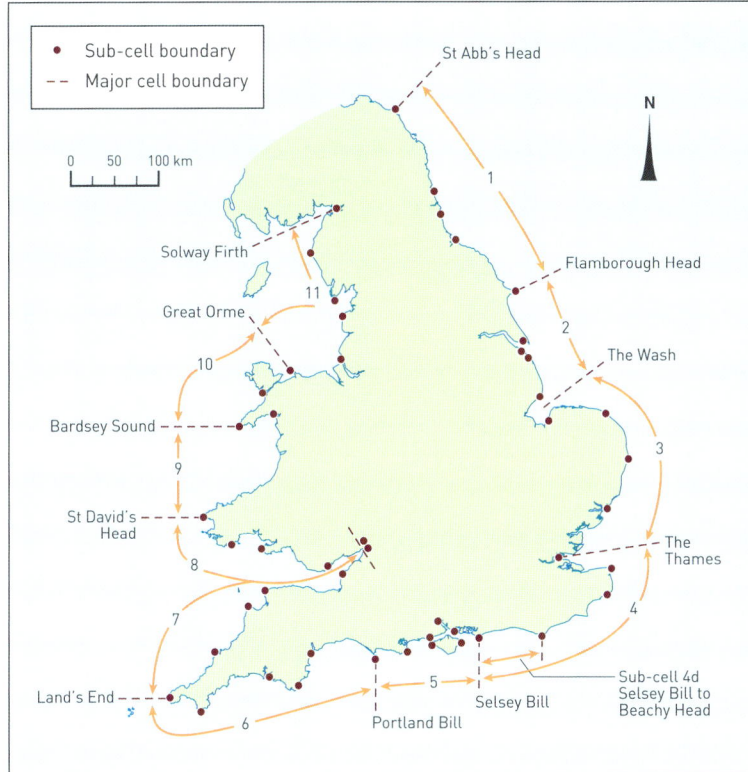

Figure 1.6 The coastal sediment cells and sub-cells of England and Wales. **Source:** Defra, 1993.

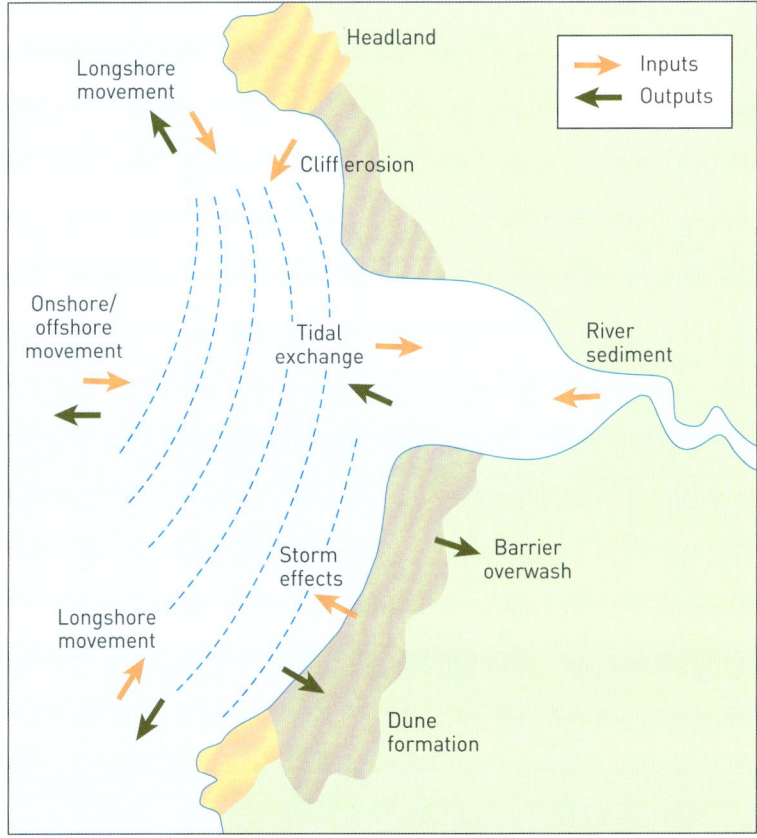

Figure 1.7 Sources and losses of sediment at an estuarine coast. **Source:** Holden, 2008.

ACTIVITY BOX 1

1. Construct a simplified system model of the coast. Identify the inputs, processes, stores and outputs and the ways in which they are connected. Does your model illustrate an open or closed coastal system? How have you indicated this?
2. Choose two coastal features and explain, with diagrams, how negative and positive feedback processes affect their development.

References

Briggs, D., Smithson, P., Addison, K. and Atkinson, K. (1997) *Fundamentals of the Physical Environment* (2nd edition). Abingdon: Routledge.

Carter, R.W.G. (1988) *Coastal Environments: An introduction to the physical, ecological and cultural systems of coastlines.* London: Academic Press.

Defra (1993) *Coastal Management: Mapping of Littoral Cells.* Available at http://eprints.hrwallingford.co.uk/748/1/SR328.pdf (last accessed 12/02/2017).

Defra (2008) *A Strategy for Promoting an Integrated Approach to the Management of Coastal Areas in England.* London: Defra. Available at www.southerncoastalgroup.org.uk/pdfs/DEFRA%20ICZM%20Strategy.pdf (last accessed 07/03/2017).

Holden, J. (ed) (2008) *An Introduction to Physical Geography and the Environment* (2nd edition). Harlow: Pearson Education.

Mediterranean ICZM Protocol (2008) 'Coastal zone policy: Protocol to the Barcelona Convention on Integrated Coastal Zone Management'. Available at http://ec.europa.eu/environment/iczm/barcelona.htm (last accessed 07/03/2017).

UNESCO/IOC (1997) *Methodological Guide to Integrated Coastal Zone Management.* Available at www.jodc.go.jp/jodcweb/info/ioc_doc/Manual/121249eo.pdf (last accessed 07/03/2017).

 Extra resources to accompany this chapter are available on the Top Spec web pages. See page 4 for further information.

2. Coastal processes

Coastal landscapes result from the interaction between coastal processes and sediment movement. Hydrodynamic (waves, tides and currents) and aerodynamic (wind) processes are important. Weathering contributes significantly to sediment transport along rocky coasts, either directly through solution of minerals, or indirectly by weakening the rock surface to facilitate further sediment movement. Biological, biophysical and biochemical processes are important in coral reef, salt marsh and mangrove environments.

Waves

Ocean waves are the principal agents for shaping the coast and driving nearshore sediment transport processes. Wind and tides are also significant contributors, and are indeed dominant in coastal dune and estuarine environments, respectively, but the action of waves is dominant in most settings. Information Box 2.1 explains the technical terms associated with regular (or sinusoidal) waves.

INFORMATION BOX 2.1 TECHNICAL TERMS ASSOCIATED WITH WAVES

Important characteristics of regular, or sinusoidal, waves (Figure 2.1).
- wave height (H) – the difference in elevation between the wave crest and the wave trough
- wave length (L) – the distance between successive crests (or troughs)
- wave period (T) – the time from one wave crest to the next wave crest measured at a fixed point. This is easy to measure in the field: simply count and time the passage of a large number of waves (at least ten) past a fixed point (e.g. a harbour wall) and divide the time by the number of waves
- wave steepness is the ratio of wave height to wavelength H/L; 'steep' waves are short and large, while 'flat' waves are long and small.

Natural waves are, however, highly irregular (not sinusoidal), and a range of wave heights and periods are usually present (Figure 2.2), making it difficult to describe the wave conditions in quantitative terms. One way of measuring variable height is to calculate the significant wave height (Hs), which is defined as the average of the highest one-third of the waves. The significant wave height off the coast of south-west England, for example, is, on average, 1.5m, despite the area experiencing 10m-high waves during extreme storms.

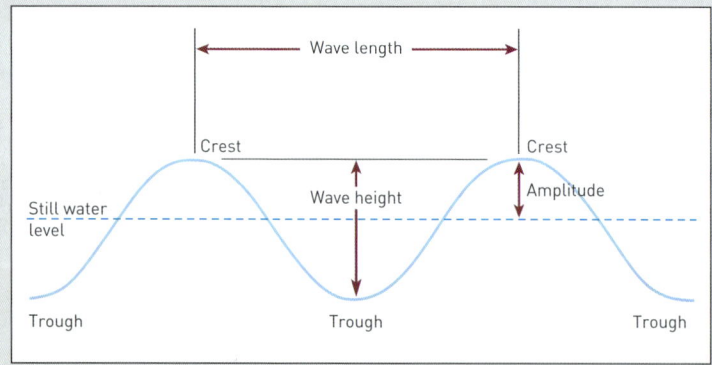

Figure 2.1 The characteristics of a regular wave.

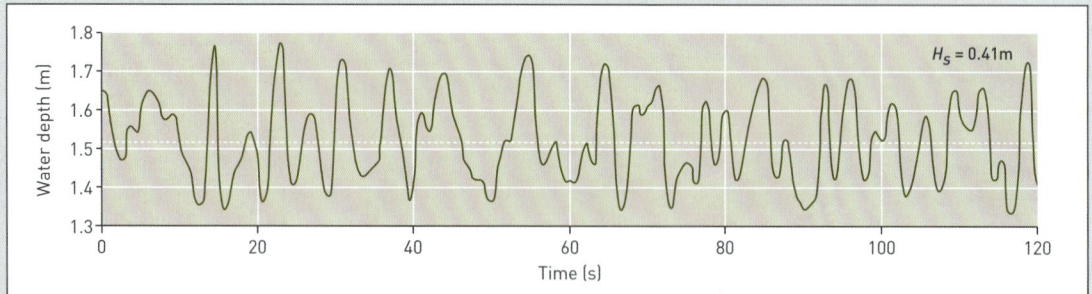

Figure 2.2 Irregular and asymmetric wave heights measured just outside the surf zone on a sandy beach over a period of two minutes. **Source:** Holden, 2008.

The size of the waves produced by a given storm depends on three factors: wind speed, wind duration (how long the wind blows for) and fetch (the distance over which the wind blows). Where strong winds blow for a long time over long distances, large waves are produced. Such waves are characterised both by their large height and by their long periods. The longer the wave period the faster the wave will be travelling. The energy carried by a wave is proportional to its height squared, thus a slightly bigger wave will have a lot more energy – a doubling of the wave height results in a fourfold increase in wave energy. In the UK, the waves with the largest fetch are those that hit the south-west coast, having travelled 7000km across the Atlantic Ocean. Large, long-period waves generated by extreme storms have incredible power, and it is this wave power that transports large amounts of beach sediment, thus changing the shape of the coast.

Waves behave differently according to the depth of water. In deep water, the waveform moves forward, but the water particles themselves have an almost closed circular motion, with virtually no forward trajectory. These circular orbits (shown in Figure 2.3) decrease in diameter with depth, until all wave motion ceases. The water depth at which the wave motion is no longer felt is known as wave base and is generally >10–20m. Beneath this, the sediment on the seabed remains undisturbed. As waves are the most significant geomorphological agent acting on the coast, causing erosion, transportation and deposition of sediment, the calculation of the wave base is critical in understanding the impact of waves along the coast.

As waves move shoreward, the water depth becomes less than the wave base, thus the seabed begins to affect the wave motion. The circular movement of water particles becomes increasingly elliptical, and eventually horizontal, and the wave length and wave velocity decrease (see Figure 2.3).

The slowing down of the wave and the shortening of the wave length causes an increase in wave height and a deformation of the wave shape that makes the waves asymmetrical and 'peaked' – this process is known as shoaling (Figure 2.4). The asymmetry of the waves means that the onshore push is stronger than the offshore pull, thus sand and gravel are driven onshore, ultimately resulting in the formation of beaches. Without this asymmetry, there would be no mechanism to transport sediments to shore.

In shallow water, waves break in a depth slightly larger than their height and the region on the beach where waves break is known as the surf zone. The wave front is too steep to maintain itself and the water particles at the crest of the wave move forward faster than the wave itself, causing collapse and the generation of bubbles and foam. Wave breaking is an important process, because when waves break, their energy is released and generates nearshore currents and sediment transport.

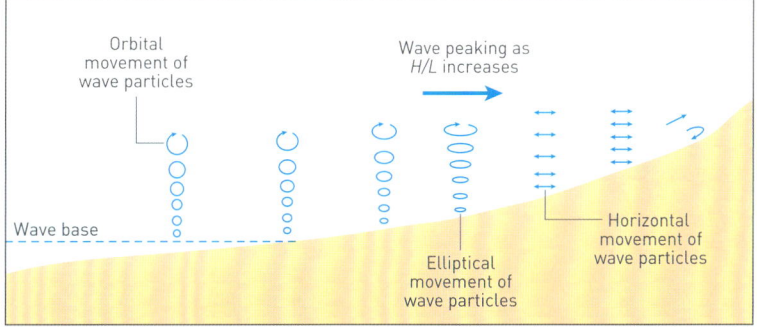

Figure 2.3 The motion of water particles under waves. **Source:** Holden, 2008.

Figure 2.4 Wave shoaling just offshore the surf zone of sandy beach. Note how peaked and asymmetric the shoaling waves are, with the wave crest being sharp and short, and the wave troughs being flat and long. **Photo:** © G. Masselink.

Wave types

A continuum of breaker shapes occurs in nature; however, three main breaker types are commonly recognised (Figure 2.5).

The type of breaker is connected with the distribution of wave energy and beach gradient. Spilling breakers are associated with wide, low-angled beaches where energy is gradually dispersed. Plunging and surging breakers often break on steep beaches soon after reaching wave base and significant amounts of energy may be reflected back to sea. When waves encounter the vertical face of a seawall, however, wave reflection approaches 100%. This may give rise to standing wave motion (clapotis) in front of the seawall and/or complicated criss-cross wave patterns where the waves arrive at an angle to the structure (Figure 2.6).

Wave refraction

Wave refraction is another important process that takes place during shoaling. It occurs where the wave front approaches the coast obliquely, and the part of the wave that is in shallower water travels more slowly than the part of the wave in deeper water. This results in a rotation of the wave crest with respect to the wave bottom contours, or, in other words, a bending of the wave rays (Figure 2.7). Refraction is an important process because it controls the angle at which the waves break. This is important for generating longshore currents and longshore drift. Drift-aligned barriers are oriented obliquely to the crest of the prevailing waves (Figure 2.7c). The shoreline of drift-aligned coasts is primarily controlled by longshore sediment transport processes, forming spits and bars (see Chapter 4).

Refraction also determines the distribution of energy along particular stretches of coast. A complex seabed topography can cause waves to be refracted in complicated ways and produce significant variations in wave height and energy along the coast. Here, wave energy is directed away from topographic depressions, referred to as divergence, which leads to relatively sheltered shoreline conditions. On the other hand, convergence, where wave energy is concentrated, will occur when waves travel over relatively shallow water (such as a sand bank on the sea floor), resulting in an increase in the wave energy and wave height (see Chapter 3).

At the shoreline, surf zone waves break onto the 'dry' beach in the form of swash. Swash motion has an onshore phase in which velocity slows (uprush), and an offshore phase characterised by acceleration under gravity (backwash). For a number of reasons (such as infiltration effects, transport of sediment within the main water flow and turbulence from the surf zone into the swash zone), more sediment is transported by the uprush than the backwash. A balance with the weaker backwash is achieved by the relatively steep gradient that generally occurs in the swash zone.

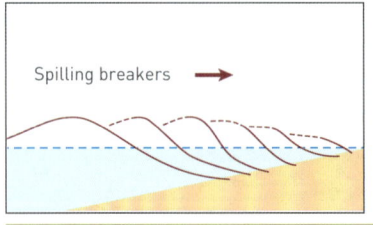

Spilling breakers are associated with gentle beach gradients and high-steepness waves (e.g. during storms). A gradual peaking of the wave occurs until the crest becomes unstable, resulting in a gentle forward spilling of the crest and the production of bubbles and foam.

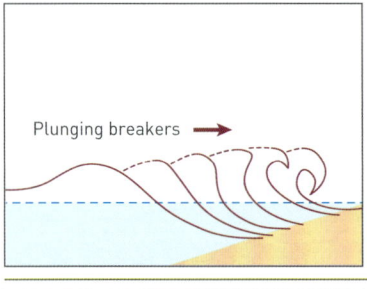

Plunging breakers occur on steeper beaches than spilling breakers, with waves of intermediate steepness. The shoreward face of the wave becomes vertical, curls over, and plunges forward and downward as an intact mass of water. Plunging breakers are the most desirable type of breaker for surfers, because they offer the fastest rides and, as they plunge over, they produce 'tubes'.

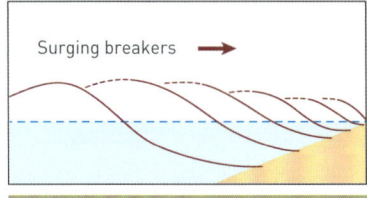

Surging breakers are found on steep beaches with low-steepness waves (e.g. summer swell waves). The front face and crest of surging breakers remain relatively smooth and the wave slides directly up the beach without breaking or producing foam.

Figure 2.5 The three main types of breakers: spilling, plunging and surging. **Source:** G. Masselink.

COASTS

Figure 2.6 Waves reflecting off a seawall at an angle, giving rise to a criss-cross wave pattern. **Photo:** © G. Masselink.

In calm conditions, the backwash returns to the sea before the next incoming breaking wave, thus there is no interference and a greater amount of sediment is transported up the beach than is brought down. In this way, steep beaches can be constructed as waves take sediment from low down the beach and deposit it at the landward edge. In stormier conditions, breaking waves and turbulent swash motion inhibit the up-beach movement of sediment and can enhance the contribution of the seaward-flowing backwash. This encourages beach erosion and results in a flattening of the beach. At the risk of overgeneralising, constructive waves tend to have a low wave steepness and destructive waves a high wave steepness.

Nearshore currents

In the surf zone, incoming wave energy is lost through noise and heat, reflected at the shore or dissipated due to wave breaking. Much of the energy from breaking waves is used for generating nearshore currents and sediment transport, ultimately resulting in the formation of distinct coastal morphology. The intensity of these currents increases with increasing incoming wave energy level – thus the strongest currents are encountered during storms. There are three types of wave-

Figure 2.7 Wave refraction: (a) The wave crest breaks on the headland while the rest of the wave continues into the bay; (b) Waves fanning out into bay but clear line of breaking waves indicates shallow depth; (c) Generation of longshore drift by refracting waves. **Photo:** surftime.ru

induced currents that dominate the net water movement in the nearshore, as seen in Figure 2.8.

Nearshore currents are capable of transporting large quantities of sediment. This is partly due to their significant flow velocities, but also because the stirring motion of the breaking waves intensifies the entrainment of sediment. The amount of sediment transported by longshore currents is known as the littoral drift and is generally of the order of 10,000–100,000m^3/yr. Such large transport rates have a major effect on coastal morphology and shoreline change.

Storm surge

Although ocean waves are the principal agents for shaping the coast and driving nearshore sediment transport, the contribution of storm surge is significant; raised water levels may last several days. During severe storms, the water level near the shore can be significantly higher than tidal predictions, and the difference between the measured and the predicted water level is the storm surge. Figure 2.9 indicates the storm surge levels observed at the Hook of Holland, January–February 1953. This disastrous storm also hit the east coast of England, causing 300 deaths (2100 deaths Europe-wide), the worst natural disaster in Europe in modern times. Under extreme conditions (such as during hurricanes or cyclones), storm surge levels can be in excess of 5m, leading to extensive coastal flooding and erosion. The maximum storm surge associated with Hurricane Katrina in the USA in 2005 appears to have been in excess of 10m.

The maximum water level at the coast during storm surge depends on four main factors:

1. The severity of low pressure – sea level will rise approximately 1cm for every 1mb fall in air pressure. Storms are always characterised by low pressure and hence the water level always rises under a storm.
2. Onshore wind – if the wind is directed shoreward it can pond water against the coast, causing an increase in the water level.
3. Coastal topography – the effect of the storm surge on the coast depends greatly on coastal configuration. Relatively low-gradient, funnel- and bay-shaped coastal settings are particularly prone to extreme surges. Examples of these are the Bay of Bengal (Indian Ocean), Gulf of Mexico (Caribbean) and the North Sea (Europe). Straight coastlines and promontories are generally less sensitive to storm surge.
4. The state of the tide – very high spring tides exacerbate the impact of a storm surge.

Tides

The tidal rise and fall of the ocean surface are barely noticeable in the deep ocean, but on shallow continental shelves, along coastlines and within estuaries, tidal processes can be the dominant morphological agent. The two driving forces for ocean tides are the gravitational attraction of the Earth–Moon and the Earth–Sun systems, with the latter having almost half the impact of the former. The theory of tides is rather complicated, therefore it is more useful to describe how tides are manifested along our coasts, than be concerned with how they are generated.

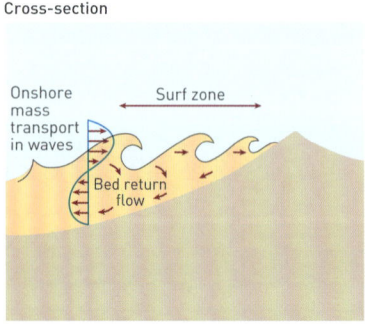

Longshore currents are shore-parallel flows within the surf zone. They are driven by waves entering the surf zone with their crests aligned at oblique angles to the shoreline; the larger the wave angle, the stronger the currents.

The **bed return flow** (sometimes misleadingly referred to as undertow) is an average flow near the bed flowing offshore. The current is part of a circulation of water characterised by onshore flow in the upper part of the water column and seaward flow near the bottom. It is the bed return flow that takes sediment eroded from the beach during storms to the edge of the surf zone where it may end up in nearshore breaker bars.

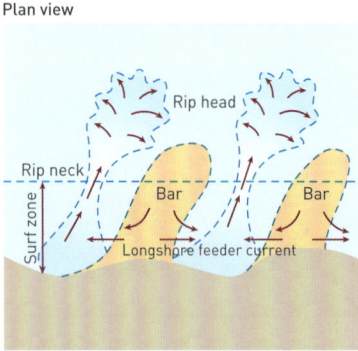

Rip currents are strong, narrow currents that flow seaward through the surf zone in channels and present a significant hazard to swimmers. As water comes onshore over bars, longshore feeder currents direct it away from the bars and into the rip itself, which transports water offshore. Maximum current velocities in rip currents may reach up to 2m/s under extreme storm conditions. Typical rip current velocities are 0.5–1m/s with flows generally stronger during low tide than during high tide.

Figure 2.8 Wave-induced currents in the nearshore – longshore, bed return flow, and rip. **Source:** Holden, 2008.

COASTS

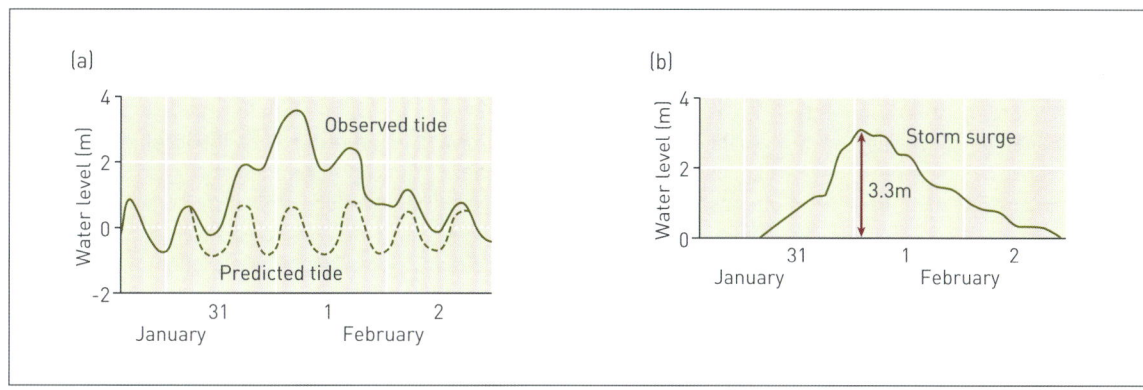

Figure 2.9 Hook of Holland, January–February 1953 (a) predicted (dashed line) tidal water level, and (b) the storm surge reached 3.3m. **Source:** Holden, 2008.

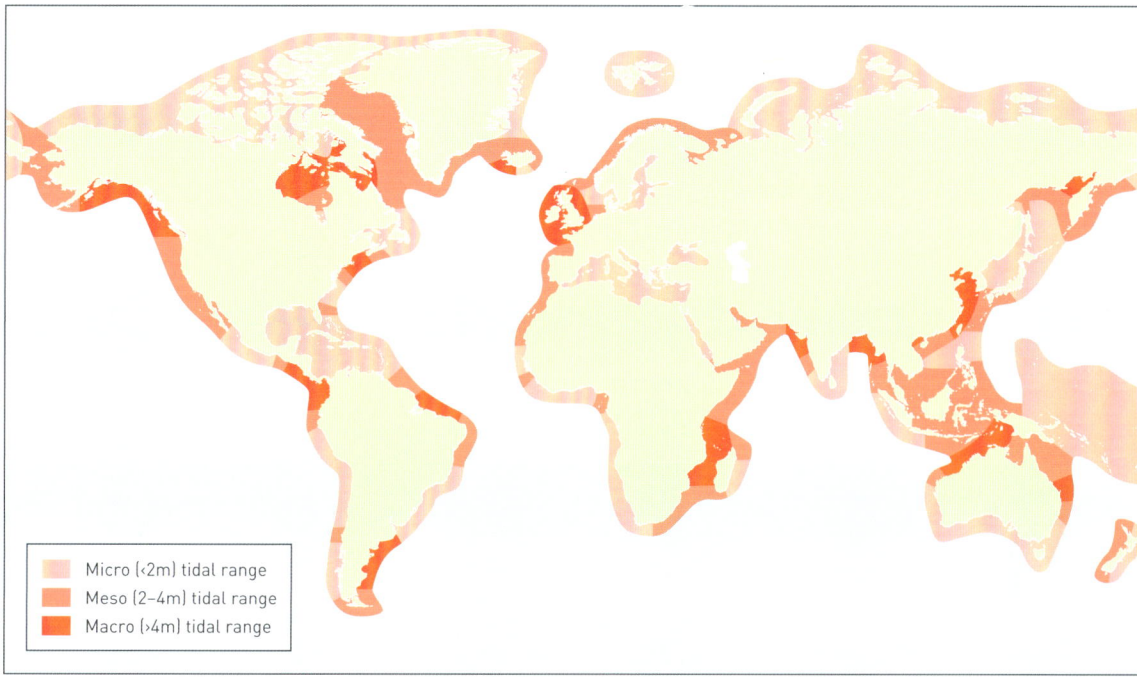

Figure 2.10 World distribution of micro, meso and macro mean spring tidal ranges. **Source:** Holden, 2008.

Along most coasts, tides cause a twice-daily rise and fall in the water level, with coasts that have mainly once-daily tides being relatively rare. The tidal range varies greatly around the world and it is common to distinguish between micro- (<2m), meso- (2–4m) and macro-tidal (>4m) ranges (Figure 2.10). The largest tidal ranges are generally associated with complex coastal configurations, such as semi-enclosed basins like the North Sea and Irish Sea, funnel-shaped bays like the Severn Estuary, and regions with wide continental shelves and island groups such as around north-west Australia.

The tidal range also varies over time, mainly due to the interaction between the tidal forces of the Earth–Moon system and the Earth–Sun system. When the Earth, Moon and Sun are all aligned, during either a full or new moon, the tidal forces of the Moon and the Sun are combined. This results in extra-large tides, known as spring tides. When the Moon is at a right angle to the Earth with respect to the Sun, however, the tidal forces of the Moon and the Sun are competing. This results in extra-small tides, known as neap tides. The Moon revolves around the Earth in 28 days; therefore, a spring-to-spring tidal cycle (or neap-to-neap tidal cycle) takes 14 days to complete.

Associated with the rising and falling tides are tidal currents whose strength increases with the tidal range. At any one place, ebb- and flood-tidal currents will vary in strength and duration. This is especially the case for estuaries (see Chapter 4). These tidal currents are important because they cause a net movement of nearshore sediment that may contribute significantly to coastal morphological development, especially where there is asymmetry in the ebb and flood flow, with currents transporting more sediment in one direction than the other.

Sources of sediment

Sediment is supplied to the coast from a variety of sources and the supply is generally intermittent, mostly occurring during storms and floods (see Figure 1.7, page 9). However, calm conditions also move sediments (admittedly at much lower rates), and such conditions are more common. Rivers erode the upland areas and bring sediment to the coast, either at estuaries or deltas where it may be deposited or become entrained in suspension, to be moved by waves or currents.

Longshore transport brings sediment from adjacent coastal cells or sub-cells (see Figure 1.6, page 9), only to be moved further along the coast by littoral (longshore) drift. In post-glacial times, offshore gravel deposits have been brought onshore, creating significant build-up such as at Chesil Beach in Dorset and Blakeney Point in Norfolk. This offshore source is now considered to be exhausted, although finer sand from offshore banks is still brought landward. Erosion of cliffs by wave attack, rainfall and groundwater seepage also contributes sediment The nature and amount controlled by the geology. The inputs from eroding cliffs can be very important for maintaining beaches downdrift of the eroding cliff sections, for example along the Norfolk coast.

Therefore, cliff erosion is not necessarily a bad thing!

The beaches around Britain range from fine sand to boulders in texture and the local lithology is reflected in shelly sand or flinty cobbles. In the mountain regions of Scotland and Wales, coarse sediments are brought down by steep-gradient rivers, whereas in lowland Britain, rivers carry mostly clay and silt. In recent decades, large-scale human intervention (including beach nourishment and construction of coastal defences) has disrupted the natural systems of sediment supply to the coast. This is why it is important, both spatially and temporally, to calculate the sediment budget for any part of the coast (Information Box 2.2; as the amount and transfer of sediment is critical in coastal management decisions.

INFORMATION BOX 2.2 SEDIMENT BUDGETS

Morphological change directly results from sediment transport processes. Sediment budgets help us to understand the different sediment inputs (sources) and outputs (sinks) involved. A sediment budget involves accounting for the sediment volumes (m^3) rather like one would account for money. Key components of the sediment budget are the sediment fluxes, which represent the direction and amount of sediment transport by certain processes and which are expressed as the quantity of sediment moved per unit of time (kg/s, m^3/yr). If the sediment fluxes are known, sediment budgets can be used to predict how the morphology changes through time in a quantitative fashion.

Consider, for example, an estuary with a surface area of 1km^2 (this is the same as 1,000,000m^2) that receives an annual input of sediment from marine and fluvial sources of 100,000m^3 per year. If it is assumed that this sediment is evenly spread over the estuary floor, then the depth of the estuary will decrease by:

$$\frac{\text{sediment input}}{\text{surface}} = \frac{100,000 \text{m}^3/\text{yr}}{1,000,000 \text{m}^2}$$

$$= 0.1 \text{m/yr}$$

If the average depth of the estuary is 10m, then the estuary will be infilled in:

$$\frac{\text{Depth}}{\text{Accretion rate}} = \frac{10\text{m}}{0.1\text{m/yr}}$$

$$= 100 \text{ years}$$

Of course, this simple illustration assumes that the amount of sediment entering the estuary does not change while the estuary is infilling. Therefore, it ignores feedback between morphology and process, which is one of the main principles of morphodynamic systems. Nevertheless, such straightforward calculations can still tell us a lot about environmental change in coastal zones. Calculation of sediment budgets lies at the heart of making predictions for future coastal development.

COASTS

Loss of sediment during storms
Storm waves can result in a loss of coastal sediment in three directions:
- Over the top. Raised water levels and large wave run-up during storms can cause waves to overtop and overwash coastal barriers, dunes and infrastructure, resulting in damage and flooding to the land behind and carrying beach material into coastal towns and onto coastal roads. This is a common response on gravel beaches. Once the beach material has been moved inland it cannot return to the beach – unless it is carried back there by human intervention using diggers and lorries.
- Offshore. On exposed beaches where storm waves approach directly (such as the west-facing beaches on the north coast of Devon and Cornwall) beach sediment is eroded from the dunes and beach by bed return flow and large rip currents (called 'mega-rips' – see Figure 2.8). These currents take the beach sand offshore into deeper water and deposit it in large sandbars in water depths in excess of 5m. The sand is gradually returned to the beach in smaller wave conditions, but, after such extreme storms, a beach may take a number of years to fully recover.
- Alongshore (Figure 2.11). On beaches where the storm waves approach at high angles, such as the south-facing beaches on the south coast of Devon and Cornwall, longshore currents drive littoral drift, transporting beach sediment alongshore. During the winter of 2013–14 the storm waves coming in from the Atlantic Ocean moved sediment from (south)west to (north)east along the English Channel causing many south coast beaches to erode at their western ends and accrete (build up) at their eastern ends. This allowed the beaches to effectively 'rotate'. For this beach material to return, a sustained period of reverse longshore drift caused by waves coming from the east is needed, although if the sediment has gone round a nearby headland, it may never return.

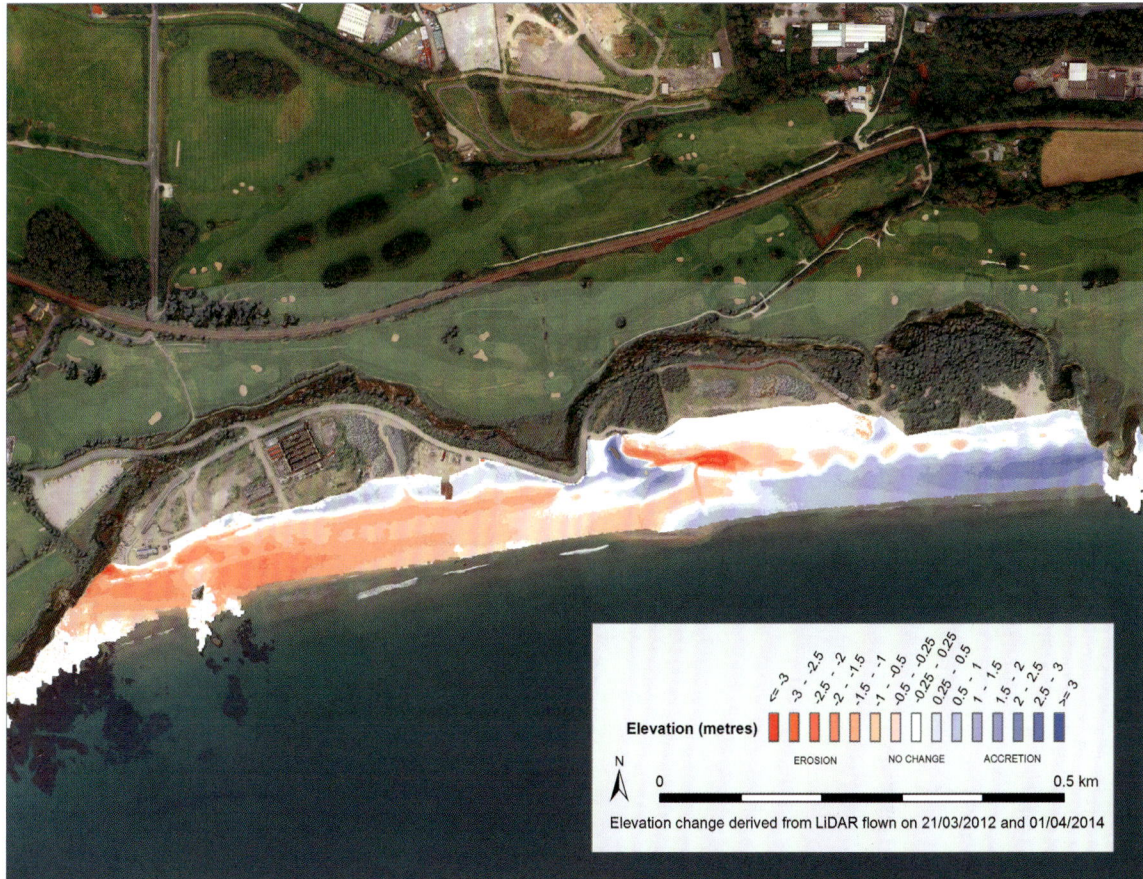

Figure 2.11 Longshore sand transport from west to east moving sand alongshore causes erosion and beach narrowing at the western end and accretion and beach widening at the eastern end. This example from Carlyon Beach, South Cornwall, shows the change in beach level before and after the extreme storms of winter 2013–14, measured using a laser (LiDAR) technique from an aeroplane. Source: Plymouth Coastal Observatory.

Measuring coastal processes during extreme storms

It has only recently become possible to make measurements of waves and coastal impacts during peak storm conditions. Over the past few years Plymouth University has developed a specialised unit, the Rapid Coastal Response Unit (RCRU), to enable the collection of data regarding extreme storm wave conditions and beach response. In addition to low tide surveys (using GPS either on foot or an all-terrain quad bike), the key instruments used are remote sensing equipment mounted above the high tide line, including digital video cameras and laser scanners, complemented by wave and current sensors deployed across the intertidal beach at low tide.

The set-up of the RCRU enables rapid deployment of video cameras with aluminium tower sections providing high and secure vantage points, and a trailer providing a mobile field laboratory. The advantage of video is that data such as how high the waves runup a beach can be remotely collected. For example, at Chesil Beach, Dorset, during Storm Petra on 5 February 2014, wave heights of up to 8m offshore resulted in vertical runup on the beach of up to 12m. That means the waves reached 12m higher (in the vertical direction) than had the sea been calm!

References

Holden, J. (ed) (2008) *An Introduction to Physical Geography and the Environment* (2nd edition). Harlow: Pearson Education.

Russell, P., Masselink, G., Scott, T., Conley D. and Davidson, M. (2015) 'Where has our beach gone? How giant waves and extreme storms impact our coast', *Geography Review*, 29, 2, pp. 2–6.

ACTIVITY BOX 2

1. Draw a spider diagram identifying the factors that control the magnitude of a storm surge.
2. Develop further the case study on the 2013–14 winter storms (available on the Top Spec web page). Go to www.geography.org.uk/resources/videocasts/impactof2013-14storms, watch the video and answer the following questions:
   - What were the specific physical and human causes of the floods during the 2013–14 storms?
   - What were the physical and socio-economic consequences of the storms?
   - Why was the cost of the damage so high? With hindsight, could any of the damage been avoided (e.g. through different infrastructure planning decisions or increased storm protection)?
   - What coastal protection strategies were in place? Were they effective?
   - How did the storms change the coastal landscape of the south-west? Have different areas been affected differently? Emphasise how changes took place over a comparatively short timescale (24 hours for each storm).
3. Assess the contribution of human activity to the sediment budget at Hallsands, near Slapton Ley in Devon (useful websites include www.slnnr.org.uk and www.abandonedcommunities.co.uk/hallsands.html).

 Extra resources to accompany this chapter, including a case study considering the sediment response to the 2014 UK storms, are available on the Top Spec web pages. See page 4 for further information.

3. Rocky coasts

Cliffs occur along approximately 80% of the world's coastline. There is a huge variety of cliff profiles and associated landforms due to the different factors and controls acting upon them, such as sea level history, geology, climate, waves and tides. The previous chapter outlined the importance of waves and tidal currents as sources of energy and agents of sediment movement, resulting in different coastal landscapes. The focus in this chapter is on rocky coasts and how the geological controls of structure and lithology, combined with energy sources and sediment transport, produce characteristic and varied rocky coastal landscapes. All rocky coasts are eroding coasts, and cliff erosion is the process by which they attempt to reach equilibrium with the dynamic driving conditions of wind, waves, tides and currents.

Rock structure

Where there is an alternating sequence of hard and soft rocks, the action of marine erosion is clearly seen, as in the classic case study area of the Isle of Purbeck in Dorset. The east-west orientation of rocks means that the southern coast is concordant ('agrees') with the structure, resulting in a fairly straight coastline formed of Portland limestone, a massive (thick strata) resistant rock (Figure 3.1a). However, at the end of the last Ice Age, when vast amounts of glacial meltwater flowed over the land, a huge river cut its way through the Portland limestone to the sea, allowing the sea to start eroding the softer Wealden beds, greensand and chalk behind, forming Worbarrow Bay and Lulworth Cove (Figure 3.1b). The almost-perfect circular shape of Lulworth Cove is due to wave refraction. The sea entrance to the cove is only 120m wide, but as waves fan out within the cove, their energy is dissipated around the bay. Erosion of the softer rocks has allowed the cove to extend back to the chalk, a relatively harder rock. Worbarrow Bay to the east has developed similarly, and has widened to more than 2km, forming headlands either side of the bay.

Stair Hole, less than half a mile away, shows how rocks were intensely folded during the Alpine orogeny – 'the Lulworth Crumple' (Figure 3.1c). It is an incipient cove, and illustrates how the bays and coves along this southern coast developed over the last few hundred thousand years. As well as forming a small arch, the sea has cut through the Portland and Purbeck limestone, causing rapid erosion of the Wealden clay behind.

The eastern coast of Purbeck cuts across the geological structure and is therefore an example of a discordant coastline (Figure 3.1d). This means that several rock types are present at the coast and their varying degrees of resistance results in differential erosion, with the formation of headlands and bays. Wave refraction concentrates erosive energy on the headlands (see Chapter 2, pages 12–13), maintaining their steep erosive morphology, but is dissipated within the bays where the more gentle waves construct depositional beaches. A major headland is Ballard Point in Dorset, where the chalk coastline is indented with many embayments. These may represent zones of multiple rock fractures, which have been eroded by wave action and abrasion by flint pebbles. North of the chalk, cut into the soft sands, is the wide, gently curving Studland Bay, and south is Swanage Bay, backed by Wealden Clay. Peveril Point marks the change to more resistant Purbeck Limestone and where the most resistant Portland Limestone occurs in the far south lies Durlston Head.

The chalk headland on the discordant coast of Purbeck has formed a classic association of caves, arches and stacks (microfeatures) at Old Harry (Figure 3.2). Initially, wave refraction would have concentrated wave energy on both sides of the headland, attacking weaknesses (such as joints and minor faults in the rock) and forming wave-cut notches. Over time, erosion enlarged these notches to form caves that were subjected to hydraulic action, loosening rock for wave quarrying. Rock falling from the cave walls and roof would have been used in the abrasion process until the cave broke through the headland, forming an arch that would have remained until sub-aerial processes (especially salt crystallisation and biological weathering), wave processes at the base and gravity acting on the rock made it unstable and it collapsed. This sequence has occurred on the chalk headland creating the stack of Old Harry. A previous stack, Old Harry's Wife, collapsed in 1896 to become a stump. The shore platform that can be seen at low tide represents an old horizontal bedding plane surface.

Elsewhere, the cave>arch>stack sequence of microfeatures may begin with the formation of a geo, where a rock weakness is eroded causing the rock above to collapse, forming a steep-sided inlet into the coast. Also, blowholes may develop in a cave, where the joints in the roof are attacked by hydraulic action and weathering until water can break through to the surface.

Rocky coast processes
Weathering
The efficiency of all erosive processes is controlled to some degree by the amount of prior weathering of the rock. Weathering

is the loosening and breaking down of rock in situ, i.e. there is no movement or erosion of rock away from its site. Many physical, chemical and biological weathering processes weaken and loosen rock material, which, once disintegrated, becomes available for removal by marine processes. Their relative importance depends principally on the climate and the rock type.

- Physical weathering is the disintegration of rock, brought about by the formation and subsequent widening of cracks in the rock. This can occur due to frost action, alternating cycles of wetting and drying, or the growth of salt crystals exerting a force within the rock.
- Chemical weathering is the decomposition of rocks, where the original state of rock minerals is changed by chemical reactions. This is most significant in hot, wet climates that promote rapid reactions.
- With biological weathering, plants contribute to the process either chemically (by dying and releasing organic acids), or physically (when roots prise their way into rock crevices). Animals also bore and produce organic acids that weather the rock chemically.

All of these weathering processes prepare the rocks for erosion, as weakened, disintegrated rock can be removed more easily.

Mass movement

Mass movements are common along rocky coasts where there are steep, and often unstable, slopes. Cliff processes and morphology depend on the following factors:

- the rock type and its resistance
- the rate of removal of debris from the cliff toe
- marine erosion processes and beach changes
- weathering
- porewater pressure.

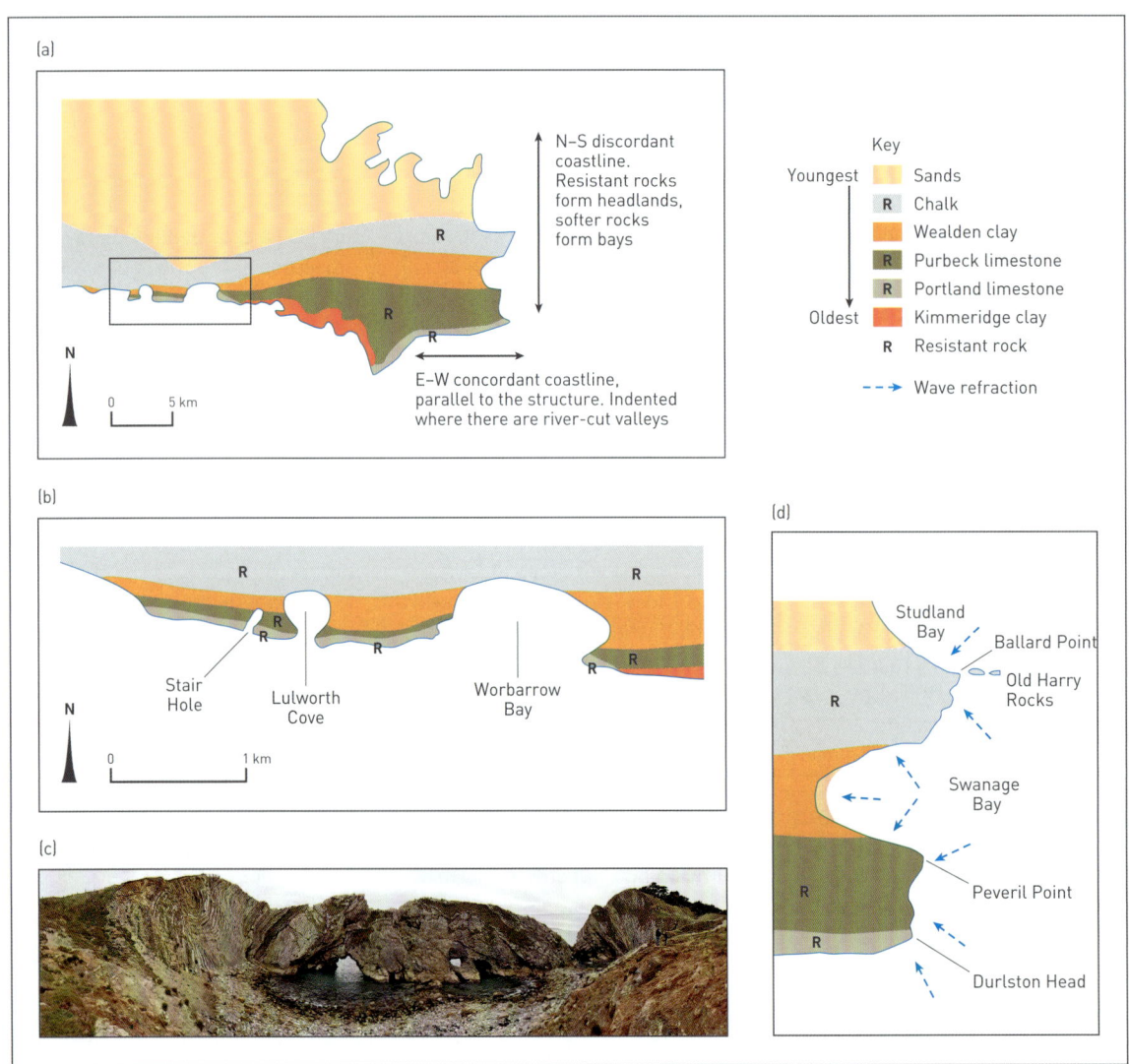

Figure 3.1 Simplified geological structure of (a) Isle of Purbeck and (b) Worbarrow Bay and Lulworth Cove; (c) Stair Hole, showing folded strata and the beginning of cove development; and (d) Refraction patterns along the discordant coast.

A good example of a gravel barrier is Slapton Sands on the south coast of Devon (Figure 1.1, p. 5), which is composed of flint pebbles that are now only found 30–40km offshore. This suggests that during postglacial sea-level rise, material has been pushed landward by a process called roll-over (see Figure 4.3).

Material is removed from the front of the barrier (the actual beach), washed over its crest (Figure 2.11, p. 17) and dumped on the back-barrier or in the lagoon (as at Slapton Ley). It is thought that this process is continuing today due to climate change and rising sea level, and that the barrier is transgressing (moving landward) at an average rate of 0.5m per year.

Beaches

Beaches consisting of unconsolidated sand or gravel deposits are the most familiar of all coastal landforms. On most beaches there are small-scale features that give a beach its distinctive morphology (Figure 4.4). A berm is a ridge at the back of the beach, marking the limit of swash action. It protects the back of the beach and coastal dunes from erosion under extreme wave conditions. The seaward part of the berm is often steep, due to onshore uprush forces often being greater than backwash forces. Energy is lost due to bed friction and infiltration of water into the beach during the uprush, particularly on coarse and permeable sediments. Therefore, the steepest berm slopes occur on gravel beaches.

Beach cusps are rhythmic scallop-shaped features on either sand or gravel beaches at the water's edge, formed by swash action (Figures 4.4 and 4.5). There are several theories relating to their formation, including that of self-organisation, as described in Information Box 4.1.

At low tide, extensive sand terraces may be exposed that may have bars and gullies parallel to the shore, on which ripple patterns may be seen. Small rip channels can be present, connecting the gullies and allowing drainage between them (Figure 4.4).

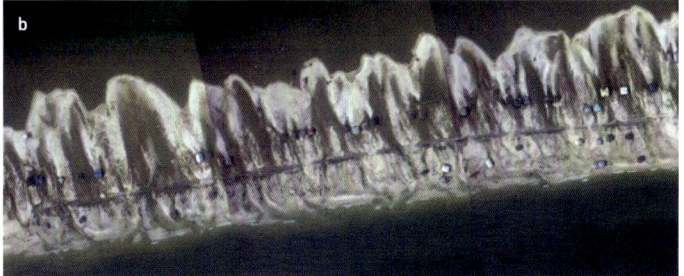

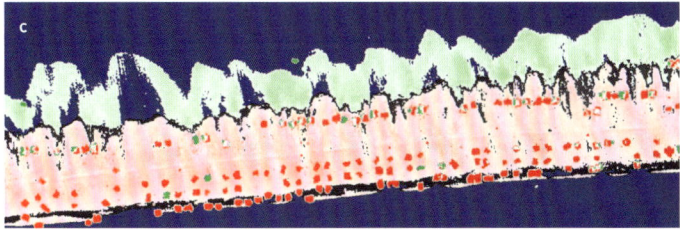

Figure 4.2 Barrier roll-over process illustrated at Dauphin Island, Alabama, during Hurricane Katrina in 2005: (a) the barrier island after the hurricane; (b) aerial view of the fan-shaped sediment; c) the morphological change during the hurricane obtained from LIDAR surveys. Pink colours represent a lowering of the beach surface and green colours represent sedimentation. The deep red squares are houses that have been destroyed and the few deep green squares are houses that have been displaced. **Source:** NASA/USGS, 2005.

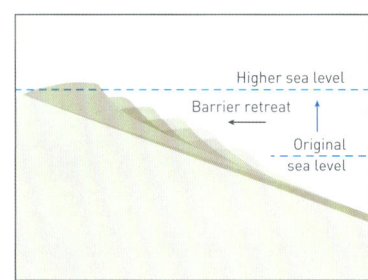

Figure 4.3 The roll-over model. Under the influence of rising sea level, sediment is eroded from the front of the barrier, transported across the barrier crest and deposited on the back of the barrier. **Source:** Masselink and Buscombe, 2008.

CHAPTER 4

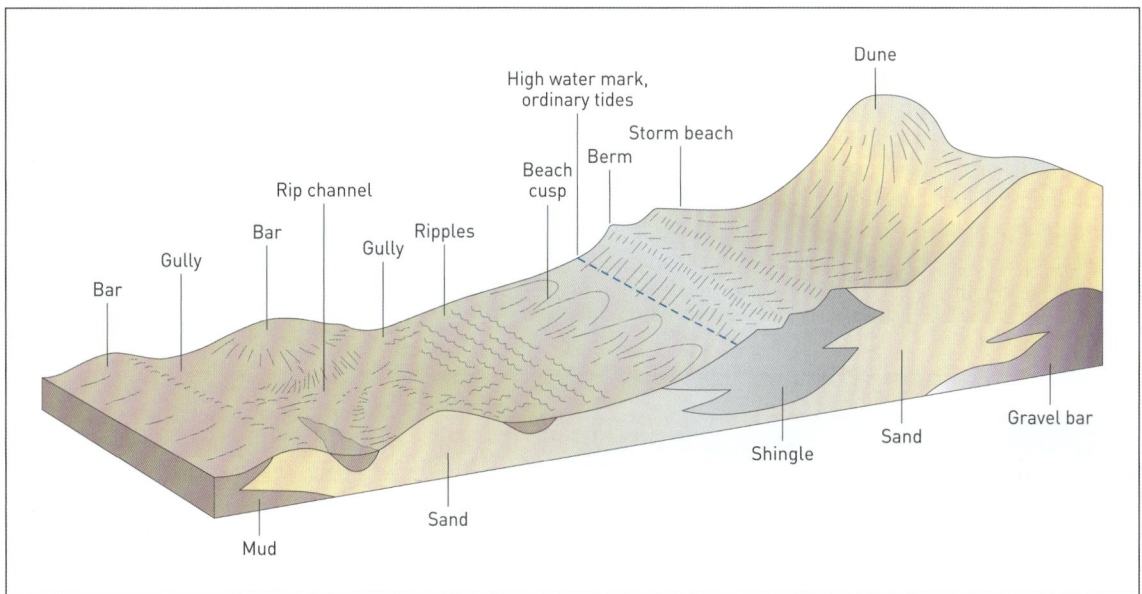

Figure 4.4 Generalised beach with small-scale features. **Source:** Briggs et al., 1997.

Figure 4.5 Gravel cusps on the Dorset coast. **Photo:** © R. Gehrels.

However, the constant wave action back and forth with the rising and falling tide, may also result in rather smooth and washed-out beach profiles. On beaches with energetic wave action, bars can also be formed beyond the low tide mark.

Beach material is very mobile, and it is this characteristic that allows beaches to withstand the roughest of storms by exhibiting resilience. Beaches are very adaptable to changing wave energy levels and of greatest significance is the exchange of sediment between the upper beach and the surf zone, and the development of berm and bar profiles (Figure 4.6). Under calm conditions, sediment transport tends to be in the onshore direction, resulting in a steepening of the beach profile. If bars are present, these tend to migrate onshore and become part of the beach, resulting in the development of a steep beach with a pronounced berm. In contrast, energetic wave conditions generate offshore sediment transport, resulting in the destruction of the berm and the formation of a flat beach with less prominent bar morphology.

Depending on the wave conditions, beaches tend to move from one beach type to the other.

INFORMATION BOX 4.1 SELF-ORGANISATION OF BEACH CUSPS

Morphodynamic coastal systems often display a sequence of positive feedback driving the system towards a new state, followed by negative feedback, which stabilises the system, resulting in equilibrium. This is referred to as self-organisation. The result of this process is a rather orderly arrangement of coastal sediments and landforms.

An example of self-organisation is the formation of beach cusps. Beach cusps are rhythmic shoreline features formed by swash action, characterised by steep-gradient, seaward-pointing cusp horns and between them, gentle-gradient, cusp embayments (Figure 4.5). The self-organisation theory of beach cusp formation considers beach cusps to be the result of feedback between morphology and swash flow.

Small topographic depressions on the beach are filled by swash, and the deeper water has a greater velocity, causing erosion. This accentuates the hollow. Conversely, as water flows over higher relief features it decelerates due to friction and deposition occurs, adding to the relief. As water flows off the cusp horns into the embayments, the backwash is concentrated, maintaining cusp morphology and equilibrium. The initially rather random and complicated interactions between beach morphology and swash action eventually results in an ordered morphological pattern. The fact that not all beaches have beach cusps indicates that their formation is a sensitive process.

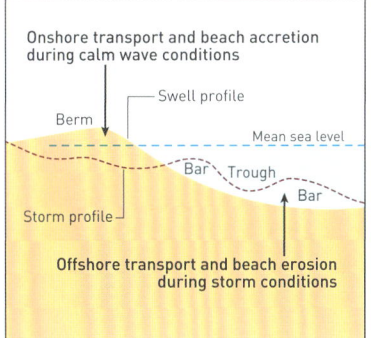

Figure 4.6 Idealised beach profiles with and without bars. Storm conditions cause offshore transport, beach erosion and the formation of a nearshore bar. Calm wave conditions result in onshore sediment transport, beach accretion and the formation of a berm. **Source:** Holden, 2008.

Along some coastlines, stormy conditions in the winter and calm conditions during summer give rise to a seasonal cycle of beach change. A beach may have a winter profile with a nearshore bar, and a summer profile with a berm, although this will vary in any given year. Regardless of whether distinctive berms and bars develop, beaches tend to be relatively wide in summer and relatively narrow in winter.

Spits

A spit is a narrow accumulation of sand or gravel, with one end (the proximal end) attached to the mainland and the other end (the distal end) projecting into the sea, or across the mouth of an estuary or bay. Spits are drift-aligned landforms that can exist only if there is a continuous long-shore supply of sediment from updrift coastal erosion or river discharge. If this sediment supply ceases, the spit will eventually disappear. Many contemporary spits have erosion issues due to a reduction in the longshore sediment supply to these systems, for example due to the trapping of sediment by groynes or the stabilisation of eroding cliffs with rip-rap.

A spit begins to develop where the coastline changes direction, such as at a headland or river estuary. The longshore current loses energy and drops some of its load on the seabed to form a submerged bank of sediment. Longshore drift continues and builds upon this base, forming an above-water spit. It continues to grow until the sediment supply is insufficient, either due to increased water depth or the erosive power of open water. If the supply is not interrupted, the spit may grow across a bay and join to the mainland again, forming a bar and enclosing a lagoon.

Wave refraction at the distal end can carry sediment around to form a curved or hooked spit. There may be several hooks visible, representing different stages of growth, as in the case of Hurst Spit in Hampshire, UK. Behind the spit, conditions are very calm and sheltered with salt marsh likely to develop. Vegetation may develop on the spit itself, thus stabilising it and enabling dune formation.

Information about the Curonian Spit on the Baltic coast can be found on the web page for this book.

Cuspate forelands

Cuspate forelands are triangular-shaped depositional features, formed by two converging longshore drift systems. Dungeness in Kent, the largest such feature in the UK, is thought to have formed due to the redistribution of shingle from former barrier beaches to the east (Hythe) and west (Fairlight – see Figure 4.7). The prevailing wind is from the south-west along the English Channel, but this is balanced by strong secondary winds from the Straits of Dover in the east.

Over time, these two systems have been in near balance, with vast shingle deposits forming a ness (or promontory) with an acute angle between the two shorelines. However, the southern beach facing south-south-west is slowly moving north and inland by the roll-over process, thus the ness point is moving south-south-east and the east-facing beach is moving further east as the ness has grown. The Dungeness coastline has necessitated a long-term beach replenishment programme (in operation since the 1950s) because the nuclear power station sited on the ness requires protection from shingle movement and rising sea levels.

Tombolos

A tombolo is most likely to form in an area with many offshore islands, but are fewer in number compared to spits and bars. St Ninian's tombolo (Figure 4.8) joins the Shetland mainland to the island of St Ninian's, making it a 'tied island'. Sand is supplied from bays to the north and south, as well as from longshore sediment transfer. As waves from the west are refracted around St Ninian's, deposition occurs in the lee of the island. It is a dynamic system, with a narrowing of the central tombolo in winter, which is reversed in summer.

Coastal dunes

Coastal dunes are formed by aeolian (wind) processes and are common features in wave-dominated coastal environments that tend to produce large sandy beaches. Dunes protect the coast from erosion and flooding by providing a buffer to extreme waves and winds. Well-developed dune systems dissipate the energy of storm waves by being eroded themselves. The sand from them will be transported offshore, but will eventually return to the beach under fair weather conditions. As the sediment is returned to the beach, wind processes may result in renewed dune development.

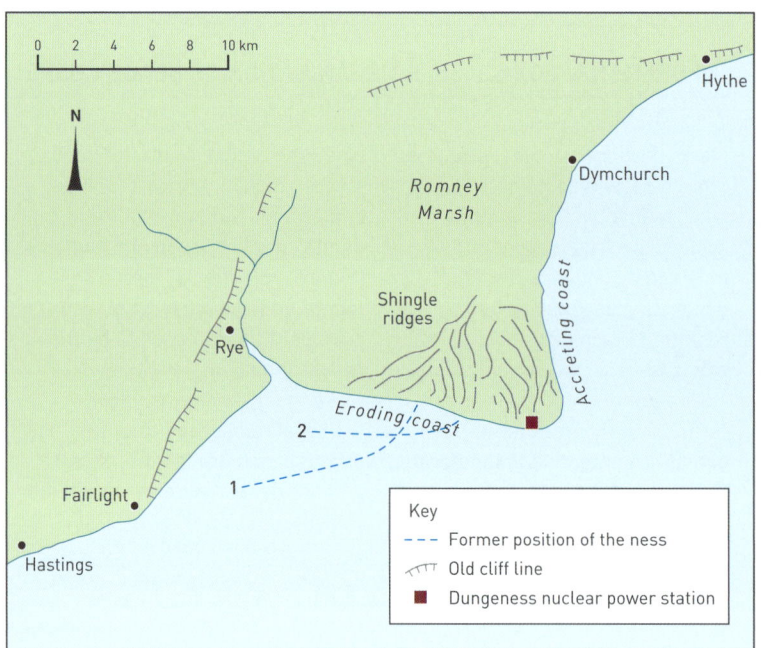

Figure 4.7 The changing cuspate foreland at Dungeness.

Figure 4.8 St Ninian's tombolo, Shetland. **Photo:** © Rob Farrow (CC BY-SA 2.0).

Maintenance of coastal dune systems is thus an important component of coastal protection and management.

Dune formation requires a number of conditions:
- space at the back of the beach on which to form
- frequent and strong onshore winds to move the sand from the beach into the dunes.

Dune height is determined by wind velocity and the highest dune systems are found in the stormiest locations, such as north-west UK (e.g. Ainsdale in Merseyside)
- a constant large supply of sand. It is common to find large dune systems close to a river that brings sediment from an eroding catchment area.

Also, if the beach in front of the dunes has a low gradient and large tidal range, this maximises the expanse of sand that can dry at low tide and be moved landward

- xerophytic vegetation (plants adapted to drought) to colonise and stabilise the dunes. Marram grass is common, and its growth is stimulated by the pressure of sand accumulation as it thrives on being buried by sand.

In strong winds sand grains may be moved in suspension, whereas gentler winds result in the sand particles bouncing up the beach, by a process called saltation. A third transport process is surface creep, where grains are rolled along the beach and dune surface by gentle winds. Coastal dunes generally begin to develop around the drift line above the spring high-tide line. Here, tidal litter (seaweed, driftwood) represents an obstacle to the wind, promoting the formation of shadow dunes with tails stretching-out downwind on the lee side. Such shadow dunes cannot reach elevations higher than that of the obstacle, but the establishment of pioneer plant species allows an ongoing accumulation of sediment. Once vegetation (such as couch grass) is present these are called embryo dunes (Figure 4.9a). Pioneer plants are specialists, all characterised by a high tolerance to salt, resistance to wind, elaborate root systems that can reach down to the freshwater table and rhizomes that grow parallel to the upper dune surface.

As embryo dunes grow upward and outward, they form foredunes about 1–2m high, that become vegetated particularly by marram grass (as at Studland, see Figure 4.9b). Given suitable conditions (onshore winds and adequate sand supply) and sufficient time, the foredunes will join together, forming a foredune ridge. Foredunes can grow quickly, reaching a height of several metres over a period of 5–10 years. Being closest to the sea, foredunes remain exposed to wind, hence the alternative term 'mobile dunes'. Foredunes protect the older dunes behind, where the sand supply is reduced and vegetation cover becomes more complete in sheltered conditions, and so these are known as fixed dunes (Figure 4.9d).

Between the ridges, where moisture collects, there may be dune slacks (Figure 4.9e). Creeping willow, flag iris and mosses thrive in these wetter conditions, where the water table is close to the surface. Occasionally, part of a dune may suffer severe erosion due to removal of binding vegetation through trampling, animal grazing or deflation, creating a blowout, a bowl-shaped depression with a flat floor (Figure 4.9c). Once the depression reaches the water table, the sand resists erosion and the surface can become re-vegetated.

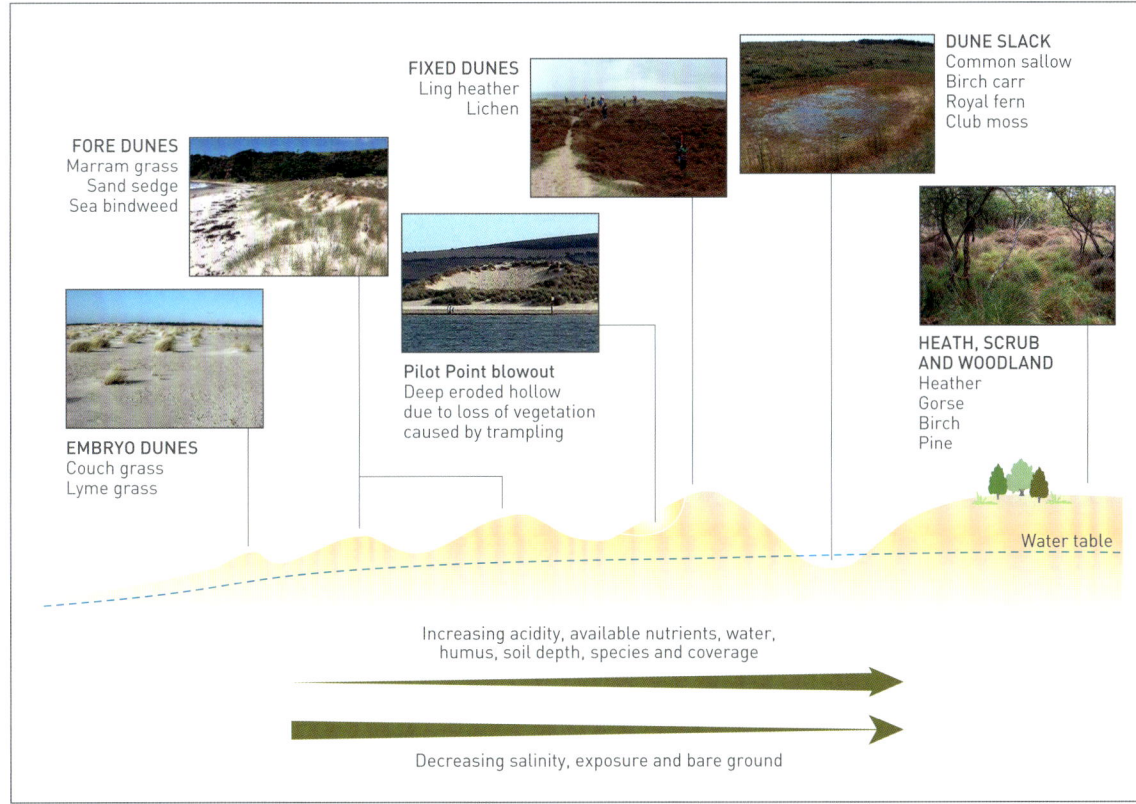

Figure 4.9 Dune development and vegetation succession (a–f) at Studland. Photos: © G. Masselink, I. West, K. Adams and G. Rogers.

At the very back of the dune system, heath develops and shrubs such as gorse invade, eventually reaching a climax community of silver birch and pine trees.

More information about the Studland dunes can be found on the web page for this book.

Estuaries

Estuaries are the main tide-dominated coastal landform. They represent zones of mixing between fluvial (river) and marine (sea) processes. The development of present-day estuaries started when coastal river valleys were flooded as sea levels rose following ice melt at the end of the last glacial period. Following stabilisation of the sea level around 6000 years ago, infilling of the estuaries started in earnest as a result of the influx of sediments from both marine and terrestrial sources. Most estuaries can be divided into three zones: an inner zone, a central zone and an outer zone (Figure 4.10). River processes dominate at the head of the estuary, but their influence decreases towards the mouth of the estuary. Marine processes are most important at the mouth, but their role decreases towards the head. The energy regime in the inner zone is, therefore, river-dominated, in the outer zone it is marine-dominated (waves and tides) and in the central zone it is mixed (tide and river processes).

Estuarine mixing is an important process occurring in estuaries. This refers to the mixing of salt- and fresh-water masses that are delivered to the estuary by tide and river flows, respectively. The mixing is accomplished by the turbulence associated with river and tidal flows and is opposed by the density difference between the two water masses – saltwater is more dense than freshwater. How the waters mix very much depends on the tidal range and the river discharge. If the tidal range is relatively small and the river discharge large, there is only partial mixing of salt- and fresh-water and the river water tends to float on the sea water. A vertical salinity gradient will be present, with freshwater at the surface, saltwater near the bed and a mixed layer in the central part of the water column. However, if the tidal range is relatively large and the river discharge small, mixing of the waters will be more effective. If the vertical mixing is very thorough there will be no salinity gradient from surface to bed, but only a gradient from outer to inner estuary. Whether an estuary is stratified or well-mixed has an important bearing on the fate of the finer sediment particles, and also the estuarine ecology.

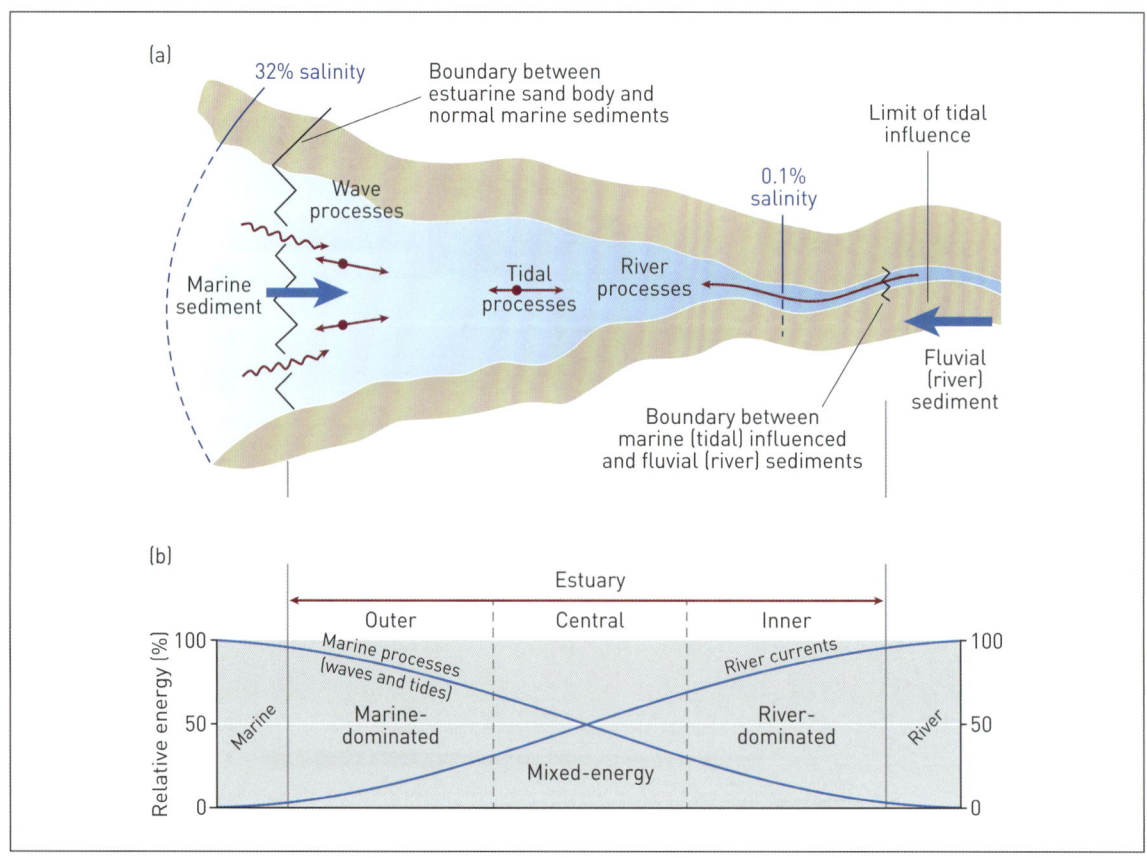

Figure 4.10 (a) Plan view of an estuary showing sediment and hydraulic boundaries; and (b) Chart showing the changing mix of wave, tide and river processes along an estuary. **Source:** Holden, 2008.

There are many types of estuaries and a popular distinction is that between tide- and wave-dominated estuaries.

Tide-dominated estuaries

Tide-dominated estuaries are found in coastal regions experiencing relatively large tidal ranges and thus strong tidal currents (Figure 4.11). The scouring action of the tidal currents keeps the entrance of the estuary open and gives tide-dominated estuaries their typical funnel shape. The strong tidal currents in the outer (marine-dominated) zone shape the sediments into linear sand bars separated by tidal channels. Waves are of secondary importance, and any influence is confined to the wider funnel mouth. Tidal energy remains relatively high throughout the estuary and a single meandering channel is commonly found in the central (mixed energy) zone. The central zone is a sink for fine sediment and includes tidal flats and salt marshes. Because tidal currents remain strong, even up to the head of the estuary, estuarine sediments can be found in the inner (river-dominated) zone, mixed with fluvial sediments.

Wave-dominated estuaries

While tide-dominated estuaries are relatively open at their mouth, wave-dominated estuaries are characterised by an outer barrier system and tidal inlet (Figure 4.12). Tides passing through the inlet constantly redistribute sediment within the central (mixed-energy) zone, forming a flood-tide delta on the landward side of the barrier, and an ebb-tide delta on the seaward side. Wave processes are dominant at the mouth, but their effects decline rapidly with distance from the inlet due to wave breaking over both the barrier and tidal deltas, leaving the central zone with lower energy levels.

Estuarine infilling

Estuaries developed as a result of the post-glacial sea-level rise and are, geologically speaking, young geomorphological features. They will eventually become infilled with fluvial and marine sediments. Once an estuary becomes completely infilled the river will flow directly into the sea and a delta will develop.

Every estuary is characterised by a unique sequence and rate of infilling. Tide-dominated estuaries mainly infill from the margins, due to tidal flat and salt marsh sedimentation and growth of the tidal sand bars in the mouth of the estuary. In wave-dominated estuaries, infilling occurs at the head of the estuary as the rivers deposit their load, fine mud particles are carried out to the central lagoon making it increasingly shallow. The expansion of the ebb and flood tidal deltas will progressively clog up the mouth of the estuary.

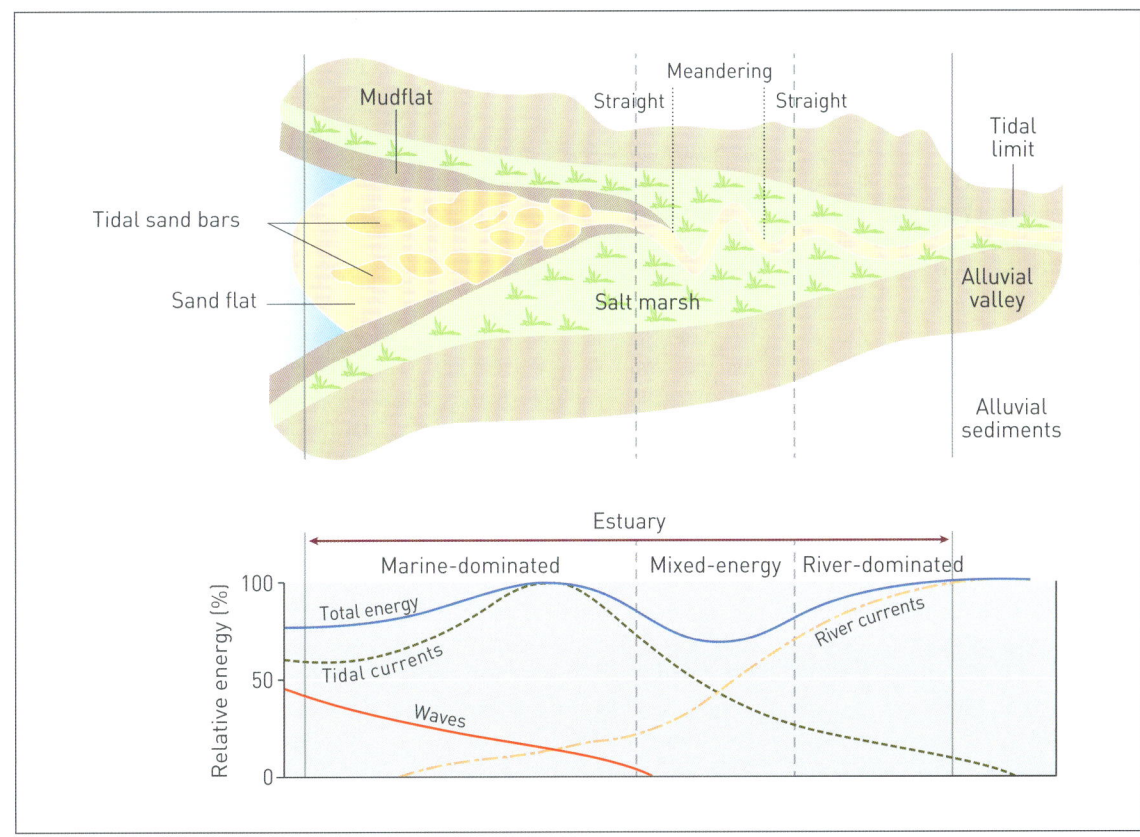

Figure 4.11 A tide-dominated estuary with an open mouth. Tidal currents contribute to relatively high energy levels throughout the estuary. **Source:** Holden, 2008.

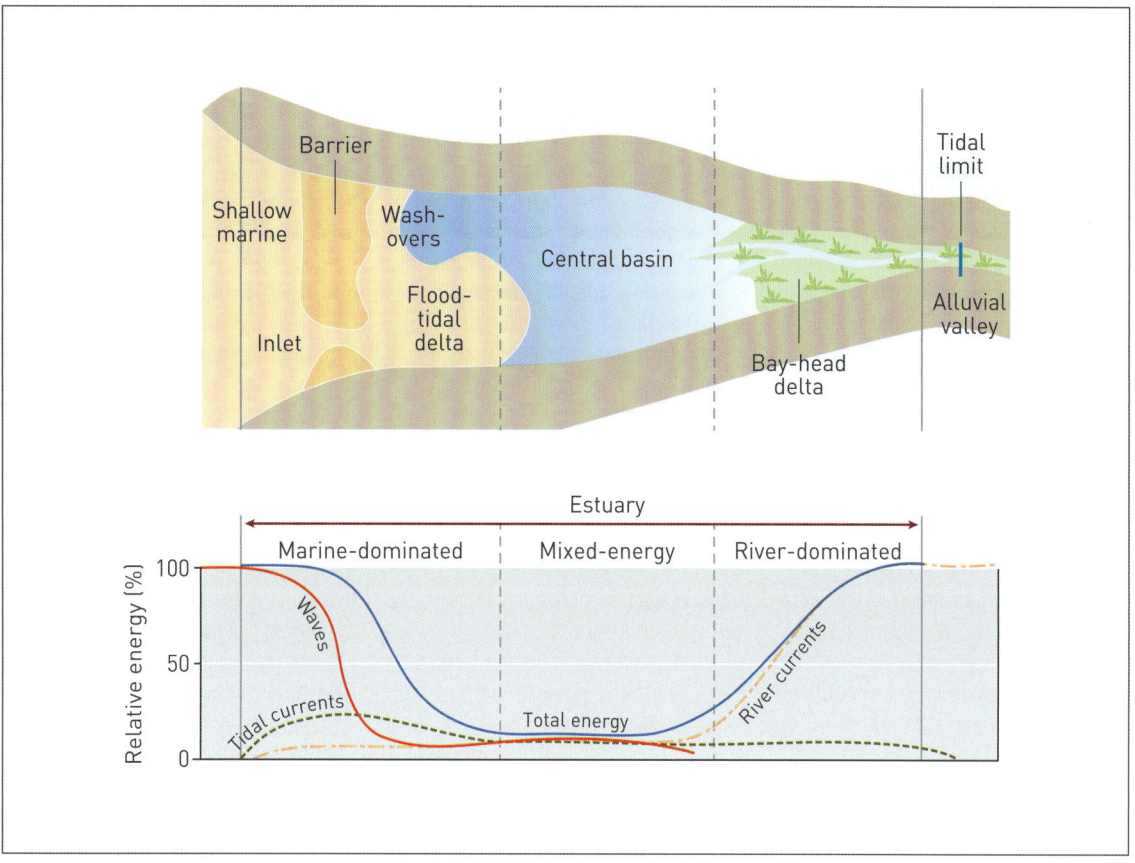

Figure 4.12 A wave-dominated estuary with barrier at the mouth. The barrier reduces wave energy in the central zone.
Source: Holden, 2008.

It is challenging to predict the rate of infill, because both ebb and flood tidal currents transport vast amounts of sediments. It is the difference between these large numbers that determines the net tidal contribution. It is easier to determine the fluvial input, but this contribution depends on the processes in the catchment, and land use plays a very significant role in determining the fluvial sediment supply.

A case study considering the differences between the Erme and Kinsgbridge estuaries in Devon is available to download from the web page for this book.

Salt marsh

As with sand dunes, salt marsh requires the interaction of geomorphological and ecological processes for their formation. The function of salt marsh in the formation of an estuary is to significantly affect the tidal flows and enhance sediment deposition of mainly silts and muds. In addition, there is a steady supply of organic detritus (roots, stems, leaves and branches) that also contributes to sedimentation. Vertical accretion rates are highly variable, both spatially and temporally, being of the order of millimetres per year. Generally, sedimentation rates exceed current and even projected rates of sea-level rise, enabling these intertidal environments to keep up with rising sea level. Salt marshes thus provide a good example of natural resilience to sea-level rise.

The lower intertidal zone in most estuaries is devoid of vegetation because there is too much wave energy preventing seedlings from taking anchor in the sediment. The upper intertidal zone is less energetic however, and here the sea has limited erosional ability. At the seaward edge of salt marsh, eel grass and glasswort are halophytic pioneers, species that spend the most time submerged by seawater. They encourage sedimentation and, as shown in Figure 4.13, when the period of inundation decreases, and the surface builds up, larger plants (such as sea meadow grass) form dense mats of vegetation and trap yet more sediment. This succession exhibits a distinct zonation, or spatial distribution of species (halosere) across the upper intertidal zone. These processes also provide a food supply for small invertebrates, which is why salt marshes are renowned for birdlife. Creeks develop in the upper marshes with rushes and reeds growing, and carr woodland develops beyond the spring high tide, with tree species adapted to wet conditions, such as alder and ash.

COASTS

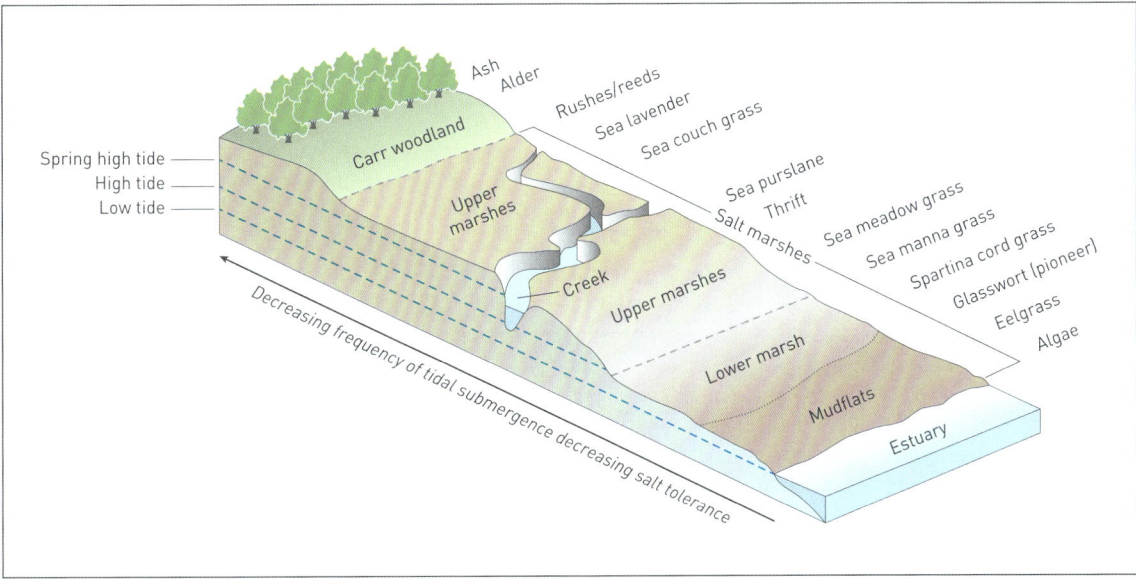

Figure 4.13 Vegetation zonation in a salt marsh. **Source:** Case, 2001.

Mangroves

Mangroves have many similar properties as salt marsh, but are found in (sub)tropical environments. They have a dense, tangled root system that slows the movement of tidal water, causing deposition during twice-daily flooding and thus the mangrove builds up its own environment. Like salt marshes, mangroves have to be adapted to low oxygen conditions, high salinity, frequent inundation and, in addition, intense sunlight. As the roots provide ecological niches for many other species, a rich biodiversity is associated with a mangrove ecosystem. Just as many UK salt marshes have conservation designations, so mangroves are often protected by national biodiversity action plans. Mangrove forests can protect the coastline from erosion, storm surges and tsunamis, by dissipating wave energy through the extensive root system. Fish are attracted by the shelter afforded by the roots and the nutrient-rich environment. The fine clay sediments attract heavy metal particles to their surfaces and act as sinks for these pollutants. Uprooting of mangroves for development can have profound negative impacts, such as during the Indian Ocean tsunami in 2004.

Both salt marsh and mangroves are very biodiverse ecosystems that link terrestrial and marine environments. They are self-sustaining through the trapping of sediment and play a vital role in protecting the coast against storms and pollution. Despite this, they are under threat from drainage and hard sea defences at their landward edge, denying them space to migrate as sea-level rises.

References

Briggs, D., Smithson, P., Addison, K. and Atkinson, K. (1997) *Fundamentals of the Physical Environment* (2nd Edition). Abingdon: Routledge.

Case, R. (2001) 'Salt marshes: Cinderellas or ugly ducklings in the coastal environment?', *Geo Factsheet*, no. 124.

Holden, J. (ed) (2008) *An Introduction to Physical Geography and the Environment* (2nd edition). Harlow: Pearson Education.

Masselink, G. and Buscombe, D. (2008) 'Shifting gravel: a case study of Slapton Sands' *Geography Review*, September, pp. 27–31.

Nasa/USGS (2005) 'Katrina rolls barrier island landward' web page: www.nasa.gov/vision/earth/lookingatearth/katrina_poststorm.html (last accessed 19/01/2017).

ACTIVITY BOX 4

1. Go to the website: http://earthobservatory.nasa.gov/Features/WorldOfChange/cape_cod.php
   It shows a series of images of changes to part of Cape Cod, Massachusetts, USA, over 30 years. Firstly, sketch the main outline of the barrier beach in 1984. Use the text to identify when major changes occurred and find the appropriate image in the sequence. Using different colours, mark each significant change of position on to your sketch. Discuss the possible reasons for these changes over time.

 Extra resources to accompany this chapter are available on the Top Spec web pages, including:
- a case study looking at the Curonian Spit, Lithuania
- further information about Studland Dunes
- a comparison of the Kingsbridge and Erme estuaries in South Devon.

See page 4 for further information.

5. Sea-level change and coastal response

As demonstrated so far, the coast is a very dynamic environment, which presents many challenges to coastal communities. The most serious threat posed to our continued use of the coastal zone is by global sea-level rise, one of the main topics addressed by the Intergovernmental Panel on Climate Change (IPCC). This large international and interdisciplinary group of leading scientists reports on the environmental and societal causes and effects of climate change, and suggests adaptive and mitigative measures. At present, global sea level is rising at an average rate of approximately 3mm/yr, with the predicted rise in sea level during this century expected to be between 28–61 and 53–98cm, depending on the emissions scenario (Figure 5.1). The main contributors to sea-level rise are shown in Figure 5.2, using observed data and models.

The two most obvious consequences of rising sea levels are coastal flooding and erosion, and the key factor that determines how severely coastal environments and communities are affected is the rate of sea-level rise. One model produced by the IPCC predicts that between 2081–2100 the rise might be in the order of 8–16mm/yr. While projections have been made up to 2100, it is virtually certain that sea level will continue to rise for centuries beyond.

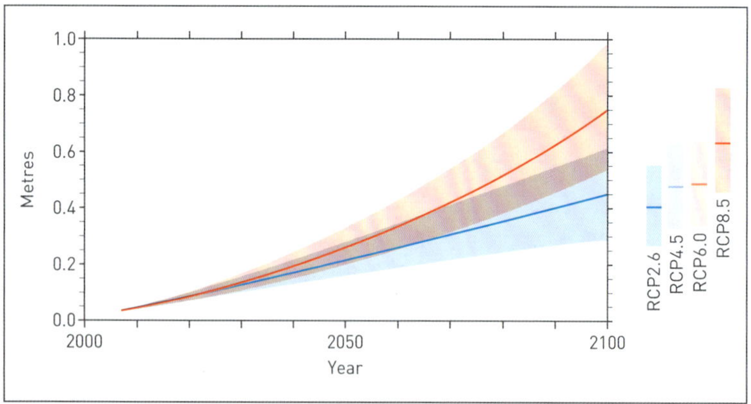

Measuring sea-level rise
To investigate trends, scientists use climate models to create future scenarios of sea-level rise. Each scenario will differ due to the data and the particular models that are used, but the important point is that all models show the same trend: one of rising sea levels (Figures 5.1 and 5.2). The shaded areas of Figure 5.1 represent the degree of uncertainty, because it is very difficult to quantify some parameters such as land-ice changes and permafrost melting. If there is very rapid melting, sea-level rise could be greater than the IPCC (2013) worst-case scenario.

Evidence of past sea-level change
Globally a wide variety of evidence indicates that sea level has varied over time.
- While erosional coasts are difficult to construct a continuous record from, because strata may be missing, erosional landforms such as fossil shore platforms, cliffs and arches can be seen above the current sea level (see Figure 5.3), or they may be submerged.
- Similarly, depositional features such as beaches and coral reefs may be above or below present-day sea level (see Figure 5.4).

Figure 5.1 Global mean sea-level rise from 2006 to 2100, according to different scenarios. The extent of the coloured area to the right of the graph shows the degree of uncertainty. **Source:** IPCC, 2013.

Source	Observed contributions to global mean sea level (GMSL) rise (mm/yr), 1993–2010	Modelled contribution to GMSL rise (mm/yr)
Thermal expansion	1.1 [0.8 to 1.4]	1.49 [0.97 to 2.02]
Glaciers (excluding Greenland and Antarctica)	1.76 [0.39 to 1.13]	0.78 [0.43 to 1.13]
Greenland ice sheet	0.33 [0.25 to 0.41]	0.14 [0.06 to 0.23]
Antarctica ice sheet	0.27 [0.16 to 0.38]	
Land water storage	0.38 [0.26 to 0.49]	
Total of contributions	2.8 [2.3 to 3.4]	2.8 [2.1 to 3.5]*
Observed GMSL rise	3.2 [2.8 to 3.6]	

Figure 5.2 Observed and modelled contributions to global mean sea level budget, 1993–2010. * Total modelled plus observed land water storage. **Source:** IPCC, 2013.

COASTS

Figure 5.3 Marine caves in cliffs on Arran, Scotland, now 8m above present day high water mark. **Photo:** © I. Johnston.

- The fossil record of organisms known to inhabit tidal zones is an indicator of old shorelines. Many submerged forests derive from 5000–6000 years ago and have since been exposed by coastal erosion.
- Submerged archaeological remains are clear indicators that sea level has risen and caused the abandonment of settlements. In Roman times, the Suffolk coastline was 2km further east than at present and, in the 14th century, Dunwich was a thriving international port, similar in size to London at that time. Rising sea levels, accompanied by increased storminess, caused coastal erosion and brought sediment to silt up the river mouth, leading to its demise as an international port in the 15th century. Dunwich now has 200 inhabitants, and the rate of change of the coastline can be seen in Figure 5.5.
- Historical documents and diaries can give details of significant recent changes.

Figure 5.4 Shell deposits within a raised beach on Rottnest Island, Western Australia. **Photo:** © G. Masselink.

Eustatic sea-level change

When there is a global change in relative sea level due to variation in the volume of seawater, it is known as eustatic change. Positive eustatic change refers to rising sea level, causing land submergence. This has occurred most recently due to the general postglacial rise in sea level resulting from the melting of ice sheets and the coasts affected are known as transgressive coasts. Negative eustatic change occurs when ocean volume decreases as temperatures fall and water is locked up on land in ice sheets and glaciers. As the shoreline recedes, it is called a regressive coastline.

35

While eustasy has occurred throughout geological time, the most important changes that can be observed along coasts today relate to the last maximum ice advance, approximately 18,000 years ago, and the subsequent interglacial (known as the Holocene) from 11,700 years BP to the present day. During the Pleistocene, between 2.6 million to 12,000 years BP, there were a series of glacial advances and interglacial cycles. As global temperatures cooled, sea level fell about 120m globally. This was because the water cycle was altered, with water stored on land as ice rather than flowing into rivers and entering the sea. As the climate warmed during interglacial periods, sea level rose, creating drowned coastlines. At the start of the Holocene, sea level rose rapidly and stabilised about 7000 years ago. Since then, sea level has risen very slowly, generally less than 1mm per year, but faster rates of eustatic change are occurring today, mainly due to human activity and the related enhanced greenhouse effect. Discussion of sea-level rise in this chapter will refer to this time period unless otherwise indicated.

Causes of eustatic sea-level rise
There are several contributing factors to the current sea-level rise, as outlined in Figure 5.2.

Thermal expansion
In any warm period, the oceans will increase in temperature. As this happens, the density of seawater decreases and the volume increases, expanding the oceans and leading to sea-level rise. According to the IPPC (2013), contemporary thermal expansion was responsible for 1.1mm/yr sea-level rise during the period 1993–2010. Variations in sea level due to changes in density are known as steric changes. Density can also be affected by variations in salinity, although these effects are more important on a local scale than globally.

Figure 5.5 The changing coastline of Dunwich, Suffolk, between 1250 and 2016. Source: D. Sear.

Melting of glaciers
Most of the valley glaciers in mountain ranges outside the polar regions have been retreating for the last 150 years. Glaciers emerge into warmer climatic zones at the foot of mountains, with vast stores of water released during melting which flow from land to ocean. Excluding Greenland and Antarctica, melting glaciers are estimated to contribute 1.76mm/yr to rising sea levels.

Greenland ice sheet
Greenland's contribution to sea-level rise is difficult to estimate. It is complicated because rising temperatures might be expected to lead to increases in precipitation at this latitude. However, the glaciers reaching the coast are receding, so accumulation may only be happening at the interior of the ice sheet. One scenario from the work of the IPCC (2013) shows that the Greenland ice sheet could melt completely over future millennia, causing sea level to rise by 7m. Its current annual contribution is estimated at 0.33mm/yr.

Antarctic ice sheet
As with Greenland, more precipitation is expected at the southern polar region and some studies show that the Antarctic ice sheet is growing annually, i.e. accumulation is greater than melting. However, the West Antarctic ice sheet is extremely vulnerable to rising sea levels because it rests on the seabed. If it becomes detached, the ice sheet will flow more quickly and thin more rapidly. The front of the glaciers will experience more iceberg calving (breaking off of huge lumps of ice), contributing to sea-level rise. At present, Antarctica is not melting as fast or as widespread as Greenland (0.27mm/year), but if the whole of Antarctica were to lose its ice in future millennia, global sea level would rise by 60m.

Surface and groundwater storage
Human usage of water and technical control over its distribution has led to changing contributions to relative sea level. Since the 1930s, numerous mega-dams have been constructed, which store water on land. Conversely, deforestation leads to faster movement of water to rivers and the coast. Pumping from aquifers has reduced groundwater stores. These changes in stores and flows in the water cycle are extremely hard to quantify and are thought to be responsible for 0.38mm/yr to sea level during the period 1993–2010.

Isostasy

Isostatic change occurs when the land moves relative to sea level, and is generally more localised. During glacial periods, the weight of ice on land can cause isostatic depression of the Earth's crust. As temperatures rise, vast amounts of meltwater enter the oceans and the land, relieved of the weight of ice upon it, rebounds and experiences isostatic uplift. As a rule of thumb, the amount of depression of the crust due to the ice is approximately one-third of the thickness of the ice. Since the thickness of the ice sheets during the glacial period generally exceeded 1km, the amount of rebound is several hundreds of metres.

During the last ice advance in the Pleistocene, ice sheets covered Scotland and northern England, creating sufficient pressure on the land to depress the crust. The mantle material that was pushed away underneath the ice sheet bulged up near the ice margin (the forebulge region). As the ice retreated, the forebulge collapsed, causing an isostatic fall in land level, and therefore relative rise in sea level. Today, the crust is currently sinking at a rate of 1mm/yr and, coupled with eustatic rise, means that relative sea level is rising in the south-east. Land in the north and west is rebounding at a greater rate than eustatic rise, thus relative sea level is falling. One can think of the UK being a relatively small crustal block that is tilting down towards the south-east, rising in the north-west, with a stable zone from the River Tees to the River Dee in North Wales (Figure 5.6).

Tectonic activity can also cause a relative rise or fall in sea level, when the crust may warp, tilt or fault under local pressure, as with the Galapagos Islands in the southern Pacific.

Coastal features resulting from sea-level change

A simple classification of emergent and submergent coasts has become established in the literature, but recent research looks to approach coastal landscapes that have undergone, or are experiencing, changing sea level in a different way. All estuaries, of which a ria is one example, are drowned features formed by the post-glacial sea-level rise, as are practically all present-day rocky coastlines, whether rias, fjords, Dalmatian coasts or other. Contemporary transgressive coastlines are now widespread due to sea-level rise, and a good example is the roll-over barrier islands or Slapton gravel barrier (Chapters 1, 2 and 4). Emergent coastlines exist only where there has been sufficient sediment added (such as deltas), or where isostatic or tectonic movement has led to a local/regional fall in sea level. It can be further complicated where emergent and submergent aspects appear in close proximity – such as in a wave-dominated estuary: the outer part with the beach, dunes and tidal inlets can be considered an emergent coastline, but the inner part clearly has the classic features of a drowned river valley.

Therefore, the following coastal features will be defined as in the classical approach, but with informed comment from current thinking.

Submerged features

Rias

During the glacial period, when the sea level was up to 120m lower and further out to sea, rivers cut down to their new base level. As ice melted, and sea level rose, the lower parts of the valleys were drowned, creating a very indented coastline.

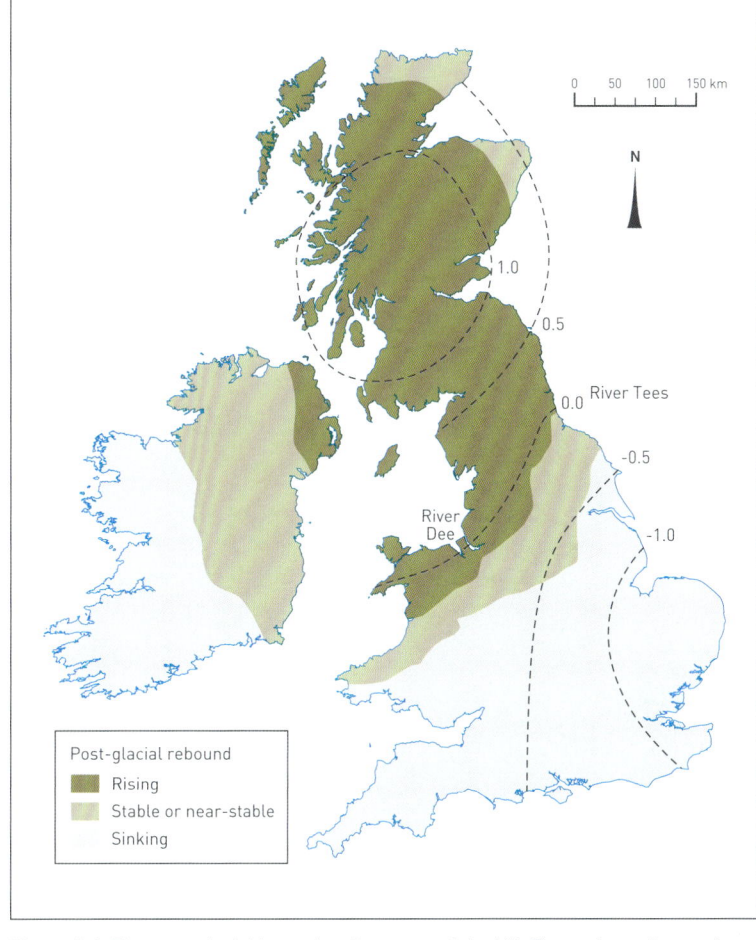

Figure 5.6 The post-glacial isostatic adjustment of the UK. The estimated rate of crustal movement is shown in mm/yr. **Source:** adapted from www.ntslf.org

Figure 5.7 Ria coastline of south-west Ireland showing the incursion of water into low-lying valleys. **Photo:** © D. Milton.

In plan view they now form a dendritic pattern (branched like a tree), and are very common in south-west England and south-west Ireland (Figure 5.7). The Kingsbridge estuary in Devon is often described as a ria, demonstrating the point that rias are a type of estuary. Rias are often presented as the quintessential drowned coastal landform, often with limited river discharge that maintains their characteristic drowned shape. If there was a lot of sediment, the estuary would become infilled (see Chapter 4).

Fjords

Fjords are over-deepened glacial troughs, formed as glaciers eroded U-shaped valleys. Again, the sea level was much lower and further away than today. The drowning of these troughs at the end of the last Ice Age means that the valley walls are extremely steep – they represent eroded truncated spurs (Figure 5.8). Fjord coastlines are found in Norway, New Zealand, Chile and Alaska. The Scottish lochs are examples of fjords, but their sides are more gently sloping. The longest fjord in Norway is Sogne Fjord, 205 km long and 1308 m at its deepest.

It could be argued that fjords are actually glacial valleys and not coastal features in themselves. They happen to occur at the coast because they were formed when sea level was lower during glacial periods. Although fjords are drowned features, and therefore a type of estuary, all areas with fjords are actually rebounding because they used to be covered with ice. One can often find raised shorelines at the head of fjords, due to isostatic rebound; whereas fjords themselves are considered submergent coasts. This is an example where the classification of features being either submergent or emergent is too simple.

Dalmatian coastlines

Where mountain ridges run parallel to the coastline (i.e. are concordant) and significant submergence occurs, the valleys are drowned, thus forming longitudinal islands and narrow channels called sounds. The name Dalmation coast is taken from a region of Croatia, which has a characteristic north-west→south-east orientation to the coastline (Figure 5.9). Note, however, that the characteristic Dalmatian coastline is not the result of particular coastal processes, but rather that it has folded rocks with the strike parallel to the coastline, that happens to be partly under water.

Lowland features

While submergence of highland areas produces distinctive coastal landscapes, flat lowland areas are also very extensive, because incursions occur far inland with only a slight slope angle. Lower valleys have become broad, shallow estuaries in the last 10,000 years (see Chapter 4). Here, deposition is dominant, providing sediment for bars, spits and marshes, and lagoons may form behind these features. Along the southern Baltic coastline, these lagoons are known as haffs.

Emerged features

If there is a relative drop in sea level, previously formed coastal features will be seen 'inland', away from the present influence of the sea. These are known as emergent or regressive coasts. Inland cliffs, sometimes with wave-cut notches or caves at their base, and with a raised beach in front (Figures 5.3 and 5.10) are common in north-west Scotland. They represent a former higher sea level. Marine platforms may also be exposed, due to isostatic rebound. The cliffs are now only subject to subaerial processes, as waves no longer reach the base to undercut them, so they have become vegetated and gentler in slope angle.

Future impact of rising sea levels on coasts

Sea-level rise and other anticipated consequences of climate change (such as increased storminess and changes to the prevailing wave direction) will impact on coastal processes. Different types of coastline respond differently to rising sea levels. Coastal environments, especially those unaffected by humans, have the capacity to cope with the impacts of sea-level rise. This ability to respond to the consequences of sea-level rise is referred to as 'resilience' and many natural features contribute to coastal resilience by providing ecological buffers (coral reefs, salt marshes and mangrove forests) and morphological protection (sand and gravel beaches, barriers and coastal dunes). A critical role in determining the resilience is played by the sediment budget. A coastline with a positive sediment budget may build up, rather than erode, under rising sea-level conditions. For example, the sediment deposition rate in salt marshes and tidal flats often exceeds the rate of sea-level rise; therefore, these environments may be able to 'keep up' with rising sea levels.

Figure 5.8 Norwegian fjord coastline, an over-deepened glacial trough drowned during postglacial sea-level rise. **Photo:** © D. Milton.

Figure 5.9 Satellite view of the Dalmatian coast in Croatia, showing drowned valleys parallel to the coast.
Source: NASA Earth Observatory, 2011.

It is expected that thermal expansion of seawater will continue, and that melting glaciers will add volume to the oceans. The polar ice masses, especially in the Arctic, are showing evidence of significant melting. A warming climate will also be expected to bring stormier weather that will particularly affect areas of softer clay. Thus, rising sea level and stormier weather will combine to act on the coasts, which will respond to new conditions of energy and sediment supply.

When considering the coastal response to rising sea level, the critical issue is whether there is accommodation space. Where there is room for sediment to move into, all coastal environments will

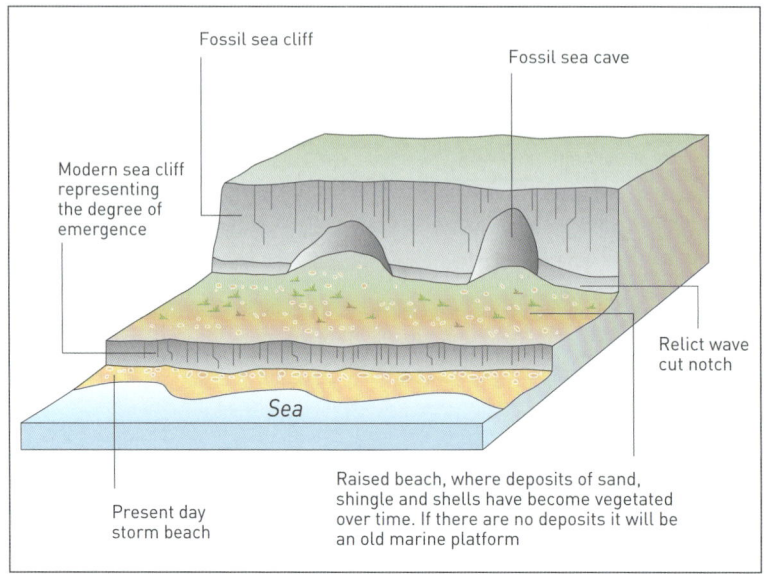

Figure 5.10 Features of a raised beach.

move landward (transgress), more or less preserving their shape and volume. Beaches are resilient if unconstrained. Where movement is restricted (e.g. by a cliff or a seawall), the environment cannot transgress and will slowly drown, with sediments moving offshore, longshore or simply submerged.

Impact on cliffs

With increased sea level rise, marine erosion at the cliff foot is likely to increase, causing undercutting, collapse and cliff retreat. The cliff will be attacked higher up its face, thus the gradient of the shore platform will change. Beaches and platforms in front of cliffs will become narrower and will drown, as the cliffs form a barrier to movement inland, and they cannot maintain their shape and volume.

Increased erosion will produce more sediment for transport along the coast, which may provide sites down-drift of eroding cliff sections with additional material to construct beaches. Abandoned cliffs may become active again as the sea reaches the foot and erosion is renewed. In north-west Scotland, where isostatic uplift is still occurring, there may be no net change in relative sea level and, therefore, no significant changes in coastal morphology.

Impact on salt marsh

The response of salt marsh (see Figure 4.13, page 34) is dependent on the sediment supply. If there is a large sediment supply, the salt marsh will prograde and build up vertically, and tidal inundation becomes a limiting factor. The salt marsh area will then become a freshwater area (usually freshwater marsh/swamp). If the rate of accretion cannot keep pace with the rise in sea level, the salt marsh will become submerged. Where rates of accretion and sea-level rise are equal, the salt marsh will exist in equilibrium. Salt marsh is particularly susceptible to coastal squeeze, where structures such as seawalls have been built behind them to protect infrastructure from erosion or flooding. This means that the marsh cannot transgress, but is eroded by waves on the seaward edge, resulting in a narrowing and eventually drowning of the salt marsh.

Impact on sand dunes

The line of foredunes (see Figure 4.9, page 30) will be eroded by the sea reaching the foot and they will become scarped. This eroded sediment returns to the beach for recycling and may be available for future dune building. Waves may break over the foredune ridge and deposit sand behind. If the whole foredune ridge is removed, the more vegetated secondary dunes become the first line of defence, but these are ill-adapted because the vegetation is not used to receiving so much salt spray and wave action. Holes may appear in the dunes with the formation of blow-outs and a degraded dune system will form. The whole dune system will move landward (transgress) if there is space behind.

Impact on gravel beaches

The crest of a gravel barrier (see Figure 4.3, page 26) could be increased as spilling waves carry material up the beach. At the same time, the crest will transgress inland, especially as the process of roll-over may be more active. Depending, again, on accommodation space, the beach will either transgress or become increasingly submerged and drown.

References

IPCC (2013) *Climate Change 2013: The physical science basis. Contribution of Working Group I to the Fifth Assessment Report of the Intergovernmental Panel on Climate Change.* Cambridge, UK, and New York, NY: Cambridge University Press. Available at www.ipcc.ch/report/ar5/wg1 (last accessed 23/01/2017).

NASA Earth Observatory (2011) 'Islands off the Croatian coast' web page: http://earthobservatory.nasa.gov/IOTD/view.php?id=50025 (last accessed 19/01/2017).

ACTIVITY BOX 5

1. Refer to Figure 5.1. Why is there such variability in scenarios of future sea-level rise? What might be the strengths and weaknesses of using different scenarios?
2. Use an atlas to identify fjord coastlines around the world. Think how they would look in plan view. Find a fjord coastline you know and then look for similar patterns elsewhere in the world.
3. Draw two annotated diagrams to show what will happen to salt marsh with rising sea levels: (a) where there is a seawall at the back protecting the land, and (b) where there is accommodation space behind the marsh. Which situation is more sustainable, and why?
4. Draw a simple diagram of the coastal system, with inputs, processes, stores and outputs. Consider how climate change and sea-level rise might impact on each component and annotate your diagram.

 Extra resources to accompany this chapter are available on the Top Spec web pages. See page 4 for further information.

6. Coastal management

Assessing the impacts of sea-level rise on our society, and formulating sustainable strategies to manage these, is obviously of great importance. An initial, and admittedly rather crude, approach is to quantify the extent of the land inundated and the number of people affected by rising sea level. Using a Digital Elevation Model (DEM) of the Earth's surface, it has been determined that for a sea-level rise of 1m, an area of 1.1 million m^2 will be flooded, which would affect 108 million people. For a sea-level rise of 2m, these numbers increase to 1.3 million m^2 and 17 million people affected. Figure 6.1 shows the importance of this by indicating the concentration of people living within 100km of coastal locations across the world.

Coastal flooding of property and infrastructure not only causes significant damage and disruption to transport, but it also intrudes into surface water and (in the longer term) groundwater supplies. In heavily populated areas such as the deltas of the Ganges-Brahmaputra (in Bangladesh and India) and Mekong (in Vietnam), and major coastal cities such as Tokyo (Japan) and Shanghai (China), human activities exacerbate subsidence, thus enhancing relative sea-level rise. Land drainage, water abstraction from aquifers, oil/gas extraction and eustatic change in sea level are all factors that have made fast-growing populations very vulnerable to relative sea-level rise. These people are dependent on flood defences and water management structures. During the 20th century, land has subsided by up to 5m in Tokyo and 3m in Shanghai. The inhabitants of small Pacific island states, such as Tuvalu and Kiribati, have already responded to sea-level rise by emigrating, and complete abandonment is a real possibility in the 21st century. Coastal managers will need to respond in advance to the threat by building appropriate defences and have to make difficult decisions as to which coastlines to defend, because it will not be technically or financially feasible to defend everywhere.

Coastlines are the most important and intensely-used of all areas settled by humans for a number of reasons, including historical settlement, trading

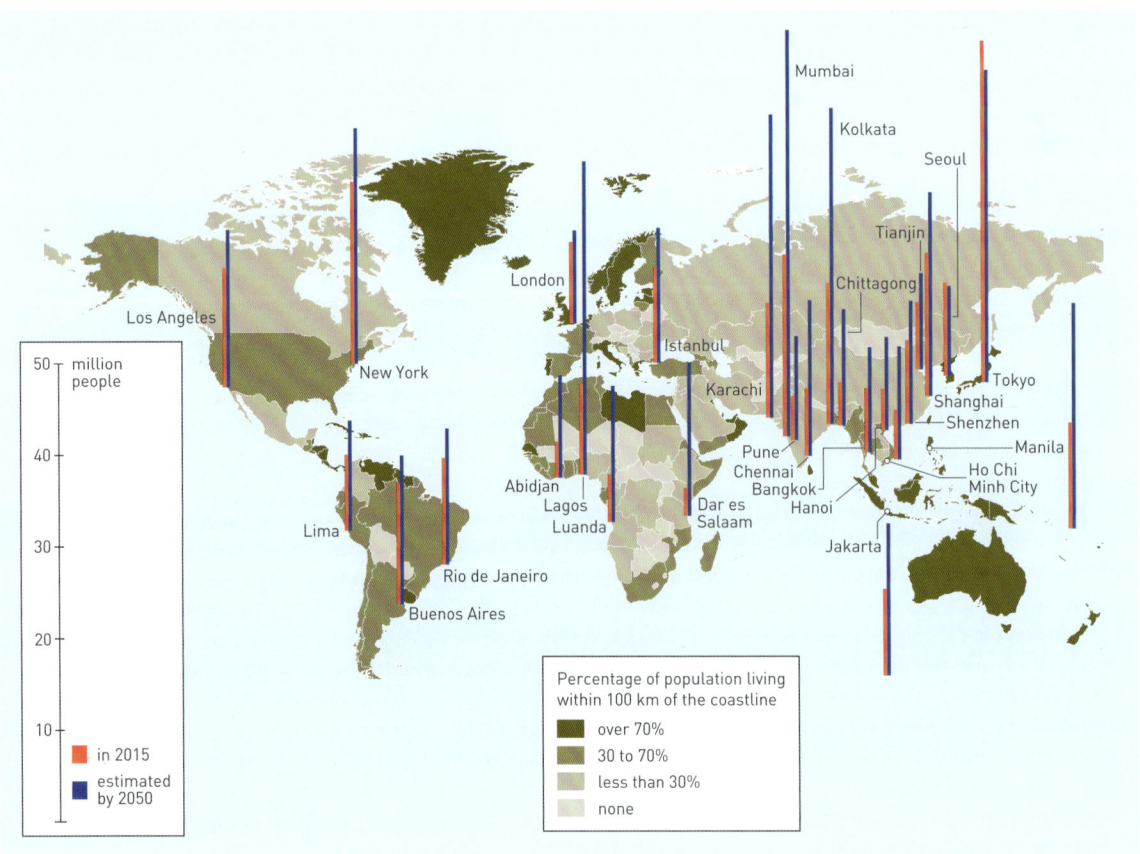

Figure 6.1 The global distribution of population, showing concentrations of inhabitants living within 100km of the coastline in 2015 and estimated future growth of coastal megacities by 2050. **Source:** adapted from GRID-Arendal/Levi Westerveld.

or political linkages, climate, availability of fertile alluvial soils, proximity to fish stocks and, more recently, aesthetic and recreational reasons. From a human point of view, the coastal zone is a resource to be used and exploited, whereas from an environmental perspective, it is an environment often adversely affected by human activities. The coastal zone is used for various activities, ranging from nature conservation to waste disposal, with most coasts supporting multiple activities. Inevitably, interactions occur between two or more coastal uses and management is required to plan and co-ordinate the different uses of the coastal zone to avoid conflicts. In the past, coastal management was mainly concerned with single issues that could be dealt with by a single authority. This is no longer the case. The increased complexity of coastal management issues, and the varying spatial and temporal scales at which they operate, bring in many different stakeholders with an interest in the management of a coastline. These typically include administrative authorities (councils, government agencies and environmental organisations), industry and other interest groups (residents and tourism). For effective management of the coast, an integrated approach should be adopted and 'integrated coastal zone management' (ICZM) is now an internationally accepted methodology (Figure 6.2).

Any ICZM initiative ought to be sustainable in order to safeguard the use of the coastal zone for future generations; thus, human activities in the coastal zone should be non-destructive and any resources we exploit should be renewable. Applying such strict guidelines, it is clear that many coastal practices are not sustainable. However, sustainability is not a set of prescriptive actions, but a 'way of thinking' about our use of the coastal zone and any resulting impacts. Generally the concept of sustainability as applied to coastal management has resulted in a management approach with a longer-term view and a more holistic perspective.

The output of ICZM consists of both legal policies and advisory initiatives (statutory and non-statutory, respectively). The latter are generally in the form of shoreline, estuarine and beach management plans, which chart out a course for the future development of a stretch of coast, estuary or beach, and/or assist in resolving current management problems. Legally binding initiatives are a powerful means to direct practices in the coastal zone.

Key principles	Comments
A broad holistic approach	A multi-disciplinary approach, taking into account both physical coastal processes and human activities, in order to ensure the long-term sustainability of communities and coastal environments.
Taking a long-term perspective	At least 50 years, and often up to the end of the 21st century (although trends will continue after this).
Adaptive management	The process of adjusting to new conditions in a way that makes individuals, communities or systems better suited to their environment. For example, the building of a seawall, beach nourishment or managed realignment.
Specific solutions and flexible measures	In a shoreline management plan (SMP), every stretch of coast is a management unit, designated with one of the four management options. For example, erosion will be allowed to continue along Cromer to Happisburgh in Norfolk, with protection of assets such as the gas terminal at Bacton, until relocation can occur.
Working with natural processes	The Sand Engine scheme, in the Netherlands. Vast amounts of sand, increasing beach height up to 5m in places, is redistributed along the coast by natural processes.
Participatory planning	All stakeholders are invited to take part in discussions and to contribute to a coastal management plan. As in Happisburgh, successful outcomes are more likely when the local community is involved in planning for the future of the coastline.
Support and involvement of all relevant administrative bodies	Many coasts have several protection designations (e.g. the Erme estuary is part of the Devon AONB, Devon Structure Plan, South Hams Local Plan, Lyme Bay and South Devon SMP and several others). Also, administrative boundaries such as local authority and parish boundaries do not correspond to sediment transport pathways. All bodies with responsibilities for any stretch of coast must be involved and agree on a plan of action.
Use of a combination of instruments	Holistic management of a complex and dynamic coastal environment will require many complementary approaches.

Figure 6.2 The key principles of the integrated coastal zone management (ICZM) methodology.

For example, the Dynamic Preservation Strategy adopted by the Dutch national government in 1991 included a legal directive that the Dutch coastline be maintained at its 1990 position, irrespective of uncertain future developments. In other words, land losses due to coastal erosion are considered unlawful and have to be compensated for by beach nourishment. On a local level, councils can use by-laws to control activities in the coastal zone; on an international level, EU legislation has played an important role in coastal management (e.g. the control of input of nutrients and chemicals into the water through the Water Framework Directive. The ICZM approach to coastal management has been adopted by an increasing number of countries worldwide, and good examples to research and compare with the UK would be Australia and Namibia (see Activity Box 6, page 51).

Shoreline Management Plans
In the UK, the whole coastline has been divided into major sediment cells (see Figure 1.6, page 9) and within these are many sub-cells, defined by sediment movement. In order for ICZM to be applied effectively, Shoreline Management Plans (SMPs) have been produced, using these sub-cells as a basis for Policy Units, to provide risk assessments associated with coastal erosion and flooding. They are also used to inform management responses in varying timescales – short (present to 20 years), medium (20–50 years) and long term (50–100 years) – and to advise on sustainable approaches, alongside other wider strategic plans. They are reviewed periodically to ensure that they remain appropriate to a changing environment and are using up-to-date knowledge. The objectives of SMPs are to:
- define, in general terms, the risks to people and the developed, natural and historic environment, within the area covered by this SMP, over the next century
- identify sustainable policy options for managing those risks
- identify the consequences of implementing these policy options
- set out procedures for monitoring the effectiveness of the SMP policy options
- identify areas that the SMP cannot address when following current guidelines
- inform others so that future land use and development of the shoreline can take due account of the risks and SMP policy options
- comply with international and national nature conservation legislation and biodiversity obligations.

SMPs do not provide details of managing the consequences of any particular coastal defence policy, such as the socio-economic impact of allowing erosion or flooding. At present, no financial compensation is given to people affected by coastal policy decisions that allow continued erosion or flooding. However, at a local level, partial or indirect compensation has been made available in some areas to help people adjust to changing conditions at the coast. In recognition of the need to support people who are affected by policy decisions, five pilot areas in the UK were chosen in 2010 to implement the 'Pathfinder' programme. This is designed to test new and innovative approaches of working with communities adapting to coastal change (see case study of the North Norfolk coast on the Top Spec web page).

Options for managing the coast
From a geographical point of view, the main issue associated with ICZM is to protect the coast from erosion and flooding. Both these aspects are particularly relevant at the moment, because 70% of our sandy coastlines are eroding and sea level is rising at an increasing rate. It is predicted that by 2029, 2000 residential properties and 15km of transport lines may be vulnerable to coastal erosion (Defra, 2011).

Within SMPs, there are four principal management options available to cope with coastal erosion and flooding due to sea-level rise. The option adopted has to meet long-term objectives, while being technically sustainable, environmentally acceptable and economically viable. In essence, it has to satisfy cost-benefit considerations (Information Box 6.1).
1. No active intervention (Do nothing) – this option is viable only if the coastline under question is undeveloped and nothing is at stake by giving up the land to coastal erosion. Examples are Fairbourne in West Wales, and Cuckmere Haven, East Sussex.
2. Managed realignment (Managed retreat) – this option involves the relocation of coastal communities and industry, with a prohibition on further development. In this strategy, risks are minimised and costs of protection are avoided. However, social and economic costs associated with relocation and compensation are potentially high (see Information Box 6.2). The retreat option requires a strong governmental role with supportive legislation. The difference between managed realignment and other soft engineering techniques is that the former involves integrated long-term planning for the delivery of many different functions. Several UK examples of this approach can be seen along the Essex coast (such as at Abbotts Hall Farm and Tollesbury), and internationally in the Rhine-Scheldt lowlands in Germany and the Netherlands, as well as in Louisiana and Texas, USA.
3. Hold the line – this option involves physically protecting the coast through hard engineering with structures such as seawalls and groynes (Figure 6.5), or soft engineering through beach nourishment, for example. A summary of coastal protection measures and the

problems associated with their implementation is given in Figure 6.3. Protection has clear social, economic and political advantages because assets and investments are safeguarded, while economic activity can continue largely unhindered. Protection is the most expensive option to implement and maintain, and it is only economically justifiable if the land to be protected is of great value.

4. Advance the line – this option is rarely applied, but occurs where sediment is applied in vast quantities, such as the Sand Engine scheme in the Netherlands. It is a form of coastal defence because it increases the resilience of the coast to erosion with its buffering capacity. Land reclamation, as used in Singapore and Hong Kong, is another example.

Accommodation and adaptation

It is now recognised that all management strategies, be they engineering structures, beach nourishment or managed realignment, are adaptive responses. Adaptation is defined as 'the process of becoming adjusted to new conditions, in a way that makes individuals, communities or systems better suited to their environment' (Defra, 2009). This understanding has led to a fifth

Management issue	Engineered solution(s)	Problems
Cliff erosion	Sea walls	
	(a) Vertical wall: a wall constructed from rock blocks, or bulkheads of wood or steel, or simply semi-vertical mounds of rubble in front of a cliff.	Rocks are highly reflective, bulkheads less so. Loose rubble, however, absorbs wave energy.
	(b) Curved wall: a concrete constructed concave wall.	Quite reflective, but the concave structure introduces a dissipative element.
	(c) Stepped: a rectilinear stepped hard structure, as gently sloping as possible, often with a curved wave return wall at the top.	The scarps of the steps are reflective, but overall the structure is quite dissipative.
	(d) Revetment: a sloping rectilinear armoured structure constructed with less reflective material such as interlocking blocks, rock-filled gabions and asphalt.	The slope and loose material ensure maximum dissipation of wave energy.
Coastal inundation	Earth banks: A free-standing bank of earth and loose material, often at the landward edge of coastal wetlands.	May be susceptible to erosion, and overtopped during extreme high-water events.
	Tidal barriers: Barriers built across estuaries with sluice gates that may be closed when threatened by storm surge.	Extremely costly, and rely on reliable storm-surge warning system (e.g. Thames Barrier).
Beach stabilisation	Groynes: Shore-normal walls of mainly wood, built across beaches to trap drifting sediment.	Starve downdrift beaches of sediment.
	Beach nourishment: Adding sediment to a beach to maintain beach levels and dimensions.	Sediment is often rapidly removed through erosion and needs regular replenishing; often sourced by dredging coastal waters.
Offshore protection	Breakwaters: Structures situated offshore that intercept waves before they reach the shore. Constructed with concrete and/or rubble.	Very costly and often suffer damage during storms.
Tidal inlet management	Jetties: Walls built to line the banks of tidal inlets or river outlets in order to stabilise the waterway for navigation.	The jetties protrude into the sea and promote sediment deposition on the updrift side, but also sediment starvation and erosion on the downdrift side.

Figure 6.3 A selection of coastal engineering works. **Source:** after Holden, 2008.

option, increasingly applied to coastal management, that of accommodation. This allows continued occupancy and use of vulnerable coastal areas by adapting to, rather than protecting fully against adverse impacts. It means learning to live with the sea-level rise and coastal flooding. Accommodation options include elevating buildings, enhancing storm and flood warning systems, and modifying drainage. The accommodation option can also involve changing activities, such as modifying farming practices to suit the new environment, or simply accepting the risks of inundation and increasing the cost of insurance premiums. The accommodation option requires high levels of organisation and community participation. It should be noted that this does not map directly onto SMP options, but is an approach increasingly used, especially in developing countries. Here, people often have no option other than to live with the risk of flooding and evacuate when a storm comes, returning when it is safe.

No active intervention, managed realignment and accommodation strategies are based on the premise that increased land losses and coastal flooding will be allowed to occur and that some coastal functions and values will be changed or lost. On the other hand, these strategies help to maintain the dynamic nature of the coast and allow it to adjust to rising sea levels naturally. It is beneficial to allow as many coastal regions to retreat as naturally as possible, because erosion of these natural areas will liberate sediments, which may lessen the impact of sea-level rise on those areas that are not allowed to retreat naturally. The overall outcome is an increase in the resilience of the coastal system to sea-level rise. Hence, the first three options are most sustainable from a geomorphological point of view (although not necessarily from a socio-economic perspective). Certainly in developed countries there seems to be an increased push by national governments to pursue these more sustainable coastal protection strategies.

Adaptation accepts sea-level rise and responds to the threats, providing both immediate and long-term local risk reduction; mitigation, on the other hand, seeks to limit the cause of long-term sea-level rise at a global scale, for example through controlling greenhouse gas emissions. Both need to be addressed in the future. The costs of adaptive measures are much lower than the costs of inaction along vulnerable coasts, especially in the developed world. Impacts on housing, businesses, infrastructure and the environment, when accounted for in a cost-benefit analysis, demonstrate the value of adaptation. Getting the balance between adaptive and mitigative approaches is problematic, because the benefits of mitigation are not immediate, thus investment in adaptive changes may be prioritised, especially in less-developed countries.

Although it is preferable to maintain the dynamic nature of coasts, there will always remain a large role for coastal protection measures for the simple reason

INFORMATION BOX 6.1 COST-BENEFIT ANALYSIS

For any coastal management decision, a cost-benefit analysis (CBA) has to be carried out. This enables decision-makers to choose the most effective form(s) of coastal protection against erosion and flooding. It attempts to put a monetary value against socio-economic costs and benefits of a particular proposal. In Figure 6.4, initial investments in risk reduction (A) result in positive net benefits (B). Further expenditure on risk reduction has lower beneficial outcomes (C), and can become negative, i.e., the cost of intervention exceeds any benefits from the work. The Environment Agency requires an average of £8 of damage avoided for every £1 spent on schemes (Committee on Climate Change, 2014). However, there are problems with this approach, because some issues (such as emotional stress) cannot be measured in monetary terms. These are known as intangibles. Costs are easier to quantify than some benefits, which can add bias to the results. If the project is carried out over a number of years, costs may change and this is complex to manage.

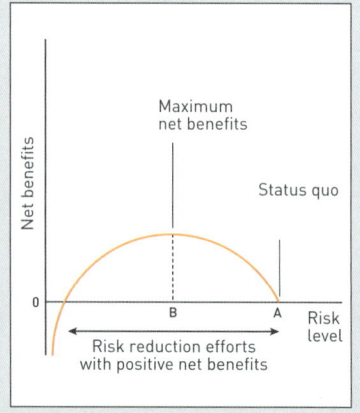

Figure 6.4 Costs and benefits model.
Source: US Army Corps of Engineers, 2014.

that many coastal areas are too valuable to be given up, and that the people living there demand defences. When properly designed and constructed, hard engineering structures do serve an important purpose: storm surge barriers (such as constructed across the Thames and in the south-west Netherlands) have prevented serious flooding on many occasions; sea walls and breakwaters protect coastal development from damage during extreme wave events; and groynes are successful to some extent in trapping sediments and maintaining a beach (Figure 6.5).

The 'side effects' of hard engineering are considerable, however, and it is well established that, following the construction of hard coastal structures, erosion problems on the down-drift unprotected coastline are often exacerbated (or even created). Soft engineering practices, in the form of beach nourishment or beach recharge, largely circumvent the main problem associated with hard engineering. The artificial placement of a large amount of sediment, either on the underwater slope or on the beach itself, protects not only the recharged coast, but also the neighbouring coastline, because sediment transport processes will redistribute the nourished sediment. However, this redistribution represents a major downside of beach nourishment because the process will have to be repeated at regular intervals, at large cumulative costs. To reduce sediment losses following beach nourishment, groynes may be placed at the boundaries of the nourished area. On the whole, beach nourishment is more aligned with sustainable coastal management and is now very widely used.

While the preceding discussion of coastal management has mostly dealt with direct impacts of coastal erosion and flooding, impacts can also be indirect. The following examples show how wide-ranging these can be – physically, biologically, economically and socially – and therefore how challenging it is to manage the coast in a holistic way.

Figure 6.5 Examples of hard engineering structures: (a) curved seawall at Dymchurch, Kent, where wave energy is forced upwards rather than directly reflected back; (b) groyne field at Christchurch Harbour, Dorset, demonstrating northward littoral drift; (c) jetties at West Bay, Dorset, designed to prevent the silting up of the harbour entrance, and (d) riprap in front of a seawall at Ryde, Isle of Wight, which dissipates wave energy and lengthens the lifespan of the seawall behind. **Photos:** © D. Milton, Google Earth.

- Groynes interrupt sediment transport, increasing or starting erosion or accretion elsewhere.
- Wetland loss affects fish populations and migratory birds.
- Polluting materials may be released from contaminated ground and landfills.
- Loss or damage to homes by erosion or flooding may affect residents' mental health.
- Land loss and frequent flooding may lead to human migration, and forced displacement in particular has negative effects.
- The value of land and the price of crops will increase as land is lost, benefiting land owners and farmers everywhere (not just in the coastal zone).
- As the price of food rises, people will have less money to spend on other things.
- Protecting against impacts will benefit the building sector and civil engineers, but reduced investment elsewhere in the economy will slow economic growth.

Recent extension of ICZM

In 2013, the European Union extended the scope of ICZM to offshore marine areas. Activities such as fisheries, aquaculture, offshore wind farms, submarine cables and pipelines and protection of marine ecosystems all have impacts on the coast. By requiring the principles of ICZM to be applied to marine spatial planning, it is envisaged that the growth of activities and the use of resources, both along the coast and out to sea, remains sustainable. It is part of the EU's Blue Growth strategy, and improved co-ordination between these two regions will reduce competition for space and pressure on valuable resources. Holistic planning under one administrative body is faster and more efficient and it is estimated that the combination of coastal and marine planning will lead to economic benefits of up to €1.6 billion across the EU.

Summary
- Effective management of the coast requires an integrated approach that considers all coastal users and stakeholders. The term 'integrated coastal zone management' (ICZM) is used to indicate this approach.
- Sustainable solutions and policies are long-term and can be applied at a number of scales.
- There are two fundamentally different types of management approaches available to approach the management of coastal erosion and flooding:
  1. strategies that allow some loss of coastal land, functions and values, but help maintain the dynamic nature of the coast (no active intervention, accommodation and managed realignment), and
  2. strategies that protect the coastline using hard and soft engineering techniques (hold and advance the line).
- Allowing coastal regions to retreat naturally increases the resilience of the coast to sea-level rise and is preferable. However, in many instances the coastline under threat is simply too valuable to be sacrificed and coastal protection must be sought.

Coastal management in wealthy and poorer countries

Human vulnerability to coastal erosion and flooding is greater in developing countries, because poor populations often lack the physical, administrative and financial resources to make adaptive responses. There may be the social and political will to protect or relocate coastal populations, but without other capacities, people remain vulnerable. In some countries that have low-lying coasts and are in hurricane tracks (such as the Philippines) much progress has been made through work on disaster management, and aid money in response to a climatic hazard has resulted in increased resilience to coastal change.

A case study comparing coastal management approaches in the Netherlands and Vietnam is available on the web page for this book.

What is the future for the coast?

Many people are divided in the degree of confidence with which they view future rising sea levels and our capacity to respond. Pessimists tend to put limits on our ability to adapt, expecting high impacts and large numbers of human displacement from coastal areas, with all the problems associated with forced migration. They point to costly adaptive measures, large population increases with growing concentrations at the coast and reactive management. Most protection in the past has been in reaction to a disaster and it will require massive foresight and political will to carry out protective measures ahead of the actual threat. The most sustainable strategies – managed realignment and accommodation – require long lead times in order to reap most benefits and need to start being put in place now, which is unlikely.

Optimists, on the other hand, believe in the ability of technology to protect coastal populations, as well as having confidence in scientific models that support the dynamic nature of the coast in adjusting to changing conditions. The Dutch even see adaptation to climate change as providing new opportunities by considering the coastal zone in a new light. Developed countries are able to demonstrate high benefit-cost ratios to prove the value of coastal protection structures. While there might be some indirect impact on economic growth, evidence from coastal megacities such as Bangkok shows that it is possible to protect and have a thriving economy. Optimists would challenge the above view that displacement from the coast is inevitable.

INFORMATION BOX 6.2 MANAGED REALIGNMENT

Managed realignment is becoming the preferred coastal management strategy in many countries. In the UK, plans exist to realign 10% of the coastline before 2030, mostly in estuarine environments or along open coast sites (Figure 6.6). The increased implementation worldwide of managed realignment is due to its adaptability in addressing the problems of rising sea levels and increased storminess associated with climate change. Techniques such as the removal, breaching and/or realignment of existing sea walls are used, although often a new line of defence has to be built inland to control the flood risk.

While it has many advantages from the perspective of flood risk managers and other environmental professionals (see Figure 6.7), other stakeholders can be more negative about such schemes. Public acceptance and stakeholder engagement with projects can be difficult to achieve, because often the gains are perceived to be entirely environmental, with economic losses borne by local people. Communication with all stakeholders is necessary to show the overall benefits of managed realignment.

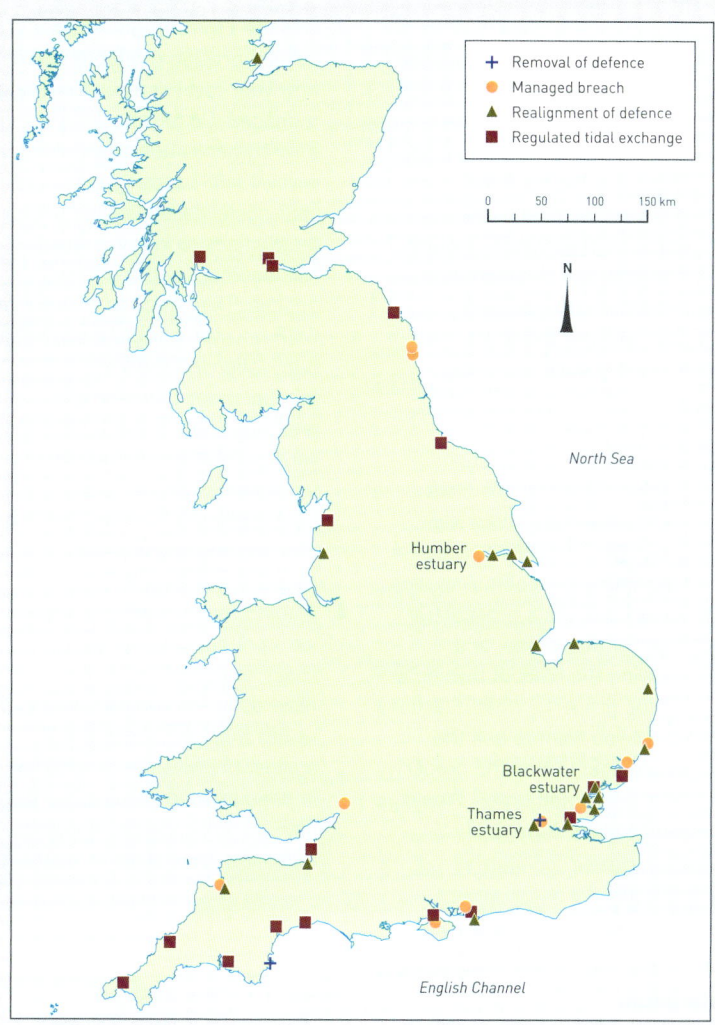

Figure 6.6 Managed realignment projects in the UK in November 2013.
Source: Esteves, 2014.

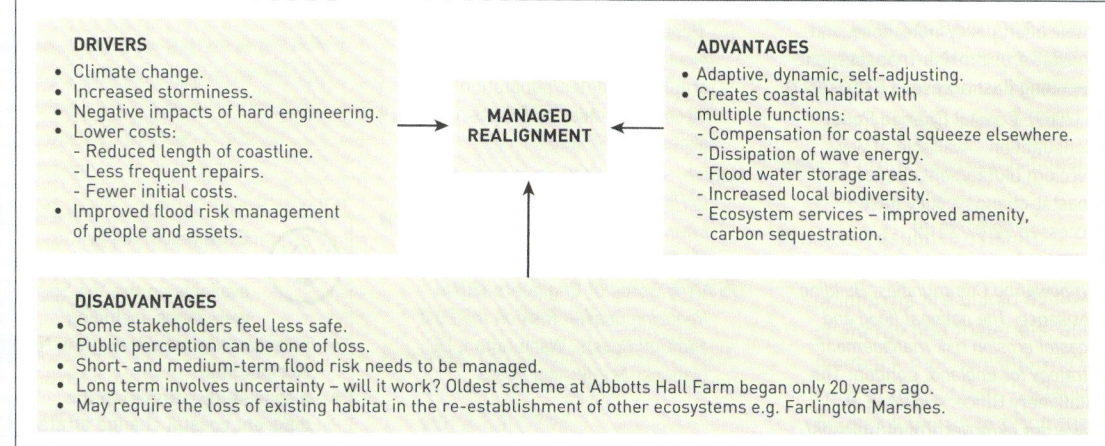

Figure 6.7 The drivers, advantages and disadvantages of managed realignment.

KEY TERMS

Prograde: to advance seaward by the building up of sediment.

Proximal: the end of the spit adjoined to the land.

Psammosere: the succession, or spatial zonation, of vegetation on sand dunes.

Regressive coast: when global temperatures fall and water is locked up on land in ice sheets and glaciers, the ocean volume decreases. As the shoreline moves seaward, progrades or builds out, it is called a regressive coastline.

Regular (sinusoidal) waves: Series of waves that is identical with constant wave height, period and length, and a sinusoidal shape.

Relaxation time: the time required for coastal morphology to adapt to a redistribution of sediment.

Resilience: the ability of the coast to respond to sea level change, such as with ecological buffers (mangroves) and depositional features (dunes, barriers).

Ria: A drowned river valley, caused by a relative rise in sea level.

Rip channel: a channel on the shore cut by a rip current flowing seaward.

Rock structure: the arrangement and alignment of rock strata.

Roll-over process: in stormy conditions, sediment is eroded from the front of the barrier, transported across the barrier crest and deposited on the back of the barrier.

Saltation: movement either by wind or water, where particles are transported by bouncing along the surface.

Salt marsh: coastal wetlands, composed of deep mud and peat, which are flooded by tidal movement.

Sediment budget: an account of the inputs, outputs and stores of sediment for a given system.

Sediment cell: a length of coastline and its associated nearshore area, within which the movement of coarse sediment (sand and shingle) is largely self-contained. Interruptions to the movement of sand and shingle within one cell should not affect beaches in a neighbouring sediment cell.

Shoaling: when waves slow down and shorten their wave length as they reach the shore, the wave height increases and the wave shape becomes asymmetrical and 'peaked' until it breaks.

Shore: the land bordering the sea, between the water's edge at low tide and the upper limit of effective wave action.

Shoreline management plan (SMP): provides assessment of the risks associated with coastal evolution and presents coastal defence policies that will achieve long-term objectives, while being technically sustainable, environmentally acceptable and economically viable.

Shore platform: an erosional surface of horizontal or gently sloping rock in the intertidal zone that has developed following erosion of a rocky coast.

Spring tide: when the Earth, Moon and Sun are all aligned, during either a full or new moon, the tidal forces of the Moon and the Sun are combined, resulting in extra-large spring tides.

Steric: refers to global sea-level change due to differences in thermal expansion and salinity levels.

Stratigraphy: The study of rock strata, primarily in sedimentary rocks.

Succession: the gradual change of species in spatial zones in an ecosystem over time, from pioneer species to climax community.

Surf zone: the zone between breaking waves and the limit of wave uprush.

Swash zone: the zone between the back shore and the surf zone, characterised by uprush and backwash.

Tombolo: is a depositional feature such as a bar or spit, which links an island with the mainland.

Trangressive coast: climate change, tectonic activity and isostasy can cause a rise in relative sea level, causing submergence, and the shore moves landward, retreats or recedes.

Weathering: the weakening and breaking down of rock material in-situ.

Xerophytic: adapted to drought.